RUGBY RENEGADE
& HOW TO PLAY RUGBY LEAGUE FOOTBALL

Gus Risman

RUGBY RENEGADE

From Rugby Union honours
to the best known personality in
Rugby League football

Scratching Shed Publishing Ltd

Rugby League Classics

This edition published by Scratching Shed Publishing Ltd, 2008
Registered in England & Wales No. 6588772.
Registered office:
47 Street Lane, Leeds, West Yorkshire. LS8 1AP

www.scratchingshedpublishing.co.uk

Rugby Renegade was originally published by Stanley Paul & Co. in 1958

How To Play Rugby League Football was originally published as part of
the Foulsham's Sports Library Series, by W. Foulsham & Co. Limited,
London, in 1938

A catalogue record for this book is available from the British Library.

ISBN 978-0956007506

Typeset in Warnock Pro Semi Bold and Palatino

Printed and bound in the United Kingdom by
L.P.P.S.Ltd, Wellingborough, Northants, NN8 3PJ

Rugby League Classics

Rugby Renegade is the first in a new series of historically significant Rugby League Classics, rescued, re-branded and re-issued in paperback, often after having been long out-of-print.

Each Rugby League Classic comes complete with at least one original manuscript intact and contains a wealth of new and updated material, including an introductory overview by a relevant writer, evocative photographs, appendices and the modern-day recollections of those closest to the book's primary subject, i.e. family members, former team-mates and other contemporary figures.

In order to stay as true to the spirit of the original text as possible, all editing has purposely been kept to a minimum. Readers should be aware, therefore, that although factual inaccuracies by the original writer - should they occur - may be referred to and corrected in the accompanying introduction, in the main text they will be allowed to stand. In the interests of readability, however, any errors in spelling and grammar (which may well have frustrated the author at the time) have now been amended, along with any inconsistencies in house style and the occasional distracting archaism.

Scratching Shed Publishing Ltd

Scratching Shed Publishing Limited is an independent publishing company founded in May 2008. We aim to produce high-quality books covering a wide range of subjects - including sport, travel and popular culture - that are of worldwide interest, yet which offer a distinctive flavour of the North of England.

Acknowledgements

The publishers gratefully acknowledge the kind assistance of the Risman family in the re-creation of this book, in particular that shown by Bev and John Risman, sons of Gus. As with their illustrious father, both are high rugby league achievers in their own right and their continued enthusiasm for and devotion to the code is a lesson to all. Truly, a couple of chips off the old block.

Thanks are due, also, to the divine Ros Caplan for making short work of the original manuscripts; Professor Tony Collins for his insight and generous help; and those friends and colleagues - too plentiful to mention - who have offered their support and good wishes to an exciting new venture.

Contents

INTRODUCTION

by Tony Collins
Professor of the Social History of Sport
Leeds Metropolitan University

Augustus John Ferdinand Risman was simply one of the greatest players ever to step onto a rugby league pitch. No-one played at the highest level for longer. No-one led international sides for longer. Only one man played more matches. Only two men played the game to a greater age. Only two men ever scored more points. And these facts are just the bare bones of his story.

But it is only when we compare Risman's career to those of great athletes of other sports that we can really get a sense of the epic achievements of the man. No-one in any other code of football can approach his longevity at the top of their chosen sport. American footballer George Blanda played for twenty-six seasons, but his last five seasons were spent as a kicker, with little to do other than come onto the field to take a shot at goal. In rugby union, Newport and Wales forward

Rugby Renegade

George Boots played for twenty-seven seasons but his international career only lasted seven years; Risman's lasted fourteen. Peter Shilton played soccer for thirty-one years but he of course was a goalkeeper.

The simple truth is that in all of the football codes around the world, there is no-one who can match Risman's record of twenty-six seasons at the very top of his sport. Gus Risman was not only unique in rugby league, he was unique in world sport. This was a truly remarkable man.

* * * * *

Like classical drama, Gus's career can be divided into three distinct acts. First came the glory years with Lance Todd's great Salford in the 1930s. Then a dual career in World War Two as an itinerant rugby league player and as an army rugby union international. And finally, transforming Workington Town from a new club to Challenge Cup and Championship winners. Any one of these periods would have been enough to cement a place in the history books, yet together they make a career that is as astounding as it is unprecedented.

As *Rugby Renegade* outlines, Gus was discovered playing club rugby union by Frank 'Bucket' Young, the great Welsh full-back who played for Leeds and toured with the first Lions in 1910. Young suggested to his former club that they might want to take a look at the young Risman but the Headingley side, with Jim Brough, the former England rugby union international, ensconced at full-back, were not interested. They were also to turn down Brian Bevan just after World War Two, so Gus was in good company.

In fact, the move to Salford could not have worked out better. Under Lance Todd, a member of the pioneering 1907 New Zealand 'All Golds' side, Salford were one of the most attractive and innovative teams in the game during the 1930s. They were noted for their brand of sparkling attacking rugby league and featured not only Risman but great players such as Alan Edwards, Emlyn Jenkins and Barney Hudson. They won the championship three times, performed a hat-trick of Lancashire Cup wins and won the Challenge Cup in 1938, which resulted in the now iconic photograph of Gus holding it aloft. Such was the thrilling nature of their rugby that the RFL chose Salford to be the first British club side to visit France in October 1934, where their style of play led the French press to nickname them the Red Devils.

When World War Two began Gus joined the Army, where he managed to pursue a dual career in club rugby league and forces rugby union. Salford closed down operations for the duration of the war in 1941 and the RFL allowed players to appear for any club as 'guests'. As his army duties took him around the country, Gus turned out for Leeds, Bradford and Dewsbury, as well as making a handful of appearances for Hunslet. In 1941 he won a war-time championship medal with Bradford and the following season won the Challenge Cup with Leeds. Thanks to the lack of restrictions on players he also played for Eddie Waring's Dewsbury team of all stars in the same season, appearing in the side that defeated Bradford in the 1942 championship final. Moreover, he made five appearances for Wales in war-time rugby league internationals.

If that wasn't enough, he also became one of the great players of war-time rugby union too, captaining the Army and Wales in union services internationals, thanks to the RFU lifting its ban on league players in the forces for the duration of the war. In an early services' match for the British Army against the Army in Ireland, *The Times'* rugby correspondent highlighted him as the difference between the two sides - the Army in Ireland, he commented, 'had nobody who could quite match the brilliance of Risman, the British Army's rugby league stand-off'.

By February 1942, *The Times* was highlighting those games in which Gus would make an appearance. The following month Wales beat England 17-12 in the first-ever services international: 'the success of Wales was largely due to their captain, A.J.F. Risman, the rugby league player, who was always dangerous in attack and very dependable in defence. He scored eight points himself and was responsible for at least one of the tries.'

The accolades continued throughout the war. At the beginning of the 1942-43 season Gus was described as 'Risman, the rugby league player whose genius has so often changed the fortunes of a game'. Service internationals continued after the war ended in 1945, most notably with a tour by the New Zealand Army which was regarded as almost a full All Black tour. The New Zealanders routed the Army 25-5 in December 1945 yet *The Times* could still single out Gus: 'Risman at right centre was brilliance itself both as a runner and a kicker'. It is worth remembering that Gus's experience of adult rugby union had ended a decade and half earlier, at the age of seventeen. To be able to walk into a rugby union match with such limited experience and take complete charge was an indication of his natural genius with an oval ball.

A similar statement could be made about the next stage in his career. When Gus returned home from the 1946 Lions tour to Australia he was no longer a Salford player but had signed up as the player-manager of the newly formed Workington Town. Cumberland had been a bastion of rugby league since the creation of the game in 1895, supporting a successful county side and supplying dozens of top-class players to clubs in Lancashire and Yorkshire, but it wasn't until the mid-1940s that it proved to be economically viable to establish professional sides in the county, firstly with Workington in 1945 and then Whitehaven in 1948. In many respects the situation resembled that which faced the Catalans Dragons many years later, as they too sought to offer elite rugby league to a regional hot-bed of the game. Gus provided both on-field leadership to the team and the charisma to give supporters belief in the side. As he recounts in *Rugby Renegade*, he inadvertently made himself a hostage to fortune by referring to a five-year plan when he arrived at the club, yet amazingly the side managed to win the championship in 1951 and the Challenge Cup in 1952. Of course, he played in both matches, the latter at the age of forty-one.

But perhaps his greatest achievements took place in the Test match arena. Gus had been the surprise selection for the 1932 Lions tour to Australia and New Zealand, winning out over Jim Brough as the reserve full-back to Jim Sullivan. He got his chance to play in the third and deciding Test in the cauldron of Sydney's SCG. The team won 18-13 to take the Ashes. His international career had begun on a high note and was to get even better. He played in twelve Ashes Test matches, was captain in seven and, as the historian Robert Gate points out in a wonderful essay in his book *Gone North*, was never dropped from the Test side. He played stand-off, centre and full-back and tasted defeat just once, in the last match of the 1937 Kangaroo tour after Britain had wrapped up the series by winning the first two Tests. He also played in five Test matches against New Zealand and won eighteen caps for Wales.

The highlight of this amazing career was his captaincy of the 1946 Lions tour to Australia and New Zealand. In 1945 he had told the Australian league journalist W.F. Corbett that he was 'too long in the tooth now' to undertake another tour, but clearly the prospect of one last crack against the Australians was too much to miss. Much has been written about how the 1946 Lions had to make their way to Australia on an aircraft carrier, the HMS Indomitable, and then had to spend days on a train crossing the Nullaboor Plain. But what is often forgotten is the deprivations that the players had to endure before they even left for Australia. The RFL issued each player with a trunk to carry their belongings down under with them, yet Gus, and probably the rest of the side too, had trouble filling it. The war had ended, yet rationing was still in operation. Clothing could only be bought if one had the right coupons, and that included sports equipment.

'I have found it difficult to obtain sufficient clothing for the trip,' Gus told the *Daily Despatch*, shortly before the tourists' departure. 'I shall travel in my demob suit [the suit issued to each soldier when they left the Army]. My football boots have been patched so often that there are now more patches than the original leather on the uppers.' His wife described to the reporter how 'it has been an awful job. I have patched and darned so that Gus could save his coupons for the tour but we have barely managed to scrape through.' When the tourists finally arrived in Australia they found themselves showered with gifts, including food parcels to send home to their families. One of Gus's regular duties as captain during the Lions' visits to the country towns of New South Wales and Queensland was to receive a symbolic food parcel of local produce that would be sent to Britain as part of Australia's support for what they still saw as the 'Mother Country', as it recovered from the war.

On the field, the 1946 tour was as fierce and competitive as anything that had gone before. On 17 June Gus led the side out onto the Sydney Cricket Ground just as he had done almost ten years previously. A twelve-man Britain held the

Australians to an 8-8 draw, after Bradford's Jack Kitching had been sent off for allegedly punching Australian captain Joe Jorgensen. In the key matches, Gus was regularly singled out for praise by the press. In the match against NSW in Sydney, *Truth* reported that he: 'showed what a fine player he is... Cool and calm, he collected the ball at will and found the open spaces with well-judged kicks. We had no counter.' In the second Test at Brisbane, which Britain won 14-5, W.F. Corbett singled him out for his 'heady deeds'. For the third Test, the teams returned to the SCG where the Australians found themselves overwhelmed 20-7. One of Australia's major problems in the last two Tests was the failure of their centres to make any progress against the British combination of Risman and Bradford's Ernest Ward. It is worth remembering that Gus had celebrated his thirty-fifth birthday shortly before the side left for Australia. When he returned almost six months later, it was as captain of the only British side ever to go through an Ashes series undefeated.

The curtain finally came down on this unprecedented career in 1954. Gus left Workington at the end of the 1953-54 season after a dispute with the club's directors and played for a few months for Batley before finally retiring in December 1954. He was 43 years, 279 days old. He had played 873 first-class rugby league matches. He had kicked 1,678 goals and scored 232 tries. No-one even knows how many appearances or points he scored in war-time rugby union.

Following his retirement, he looked certain to become one of the game's great coaches. But it was not to be. Eddie Waring in his warm and generous tribute to Gus in his book, *The Great Ones*, described how he too thought that Risman would be 'a natural as a manager, but he was unable to click as he had done as a player-manager'. Perhaps it was his very longevity as a player that made it difficult for him to connect with players when he could no longer lead by example. There are passages in *Rugby Renegade* where he makes clear his belief that the game in the 1950s was not as advanced as in the 1930s. His stints at Salford, Bradford and Oldham were sadly undistinguished. At Oldham, where he had a short spell as manager in the late 1950s, it seems that players found him aloof. Whether this was a generational gap or the problem of the prodigiously gifted player trying to instruct those who were less talented is unclear. Sadly, as a manager he was never able to develop the rapport with players which he had when he played. Unlike his great rival Jim Sullivan he was never to become the great coach that everyone in the game expected him to be. Maybe having the equivalent of three great careers was enough for one mortal.

* * * * *

The two books reprinted here are landmarks in themselves. *How To Play Rugby League Football* appeared in 1938 and was the first book about the game ever to be produced by a national publisher.

In contrast to the huge numbers of books about soccer and rugby union, it had taken almost fifty years for a publisher to recognise the interest in rugby league. Even Harold Wagstaff's autobiography had only been published in weekly parts in a local newspaper. And another two decades would pass before the next nationally published rugby league book in 1958. The fact that it, too, was by Gus is testimony to his longevity and standing in the game. *Rugby Renegade* was part of the publisher Stanley Paul's burgeoning line of sports books. It was ghost-written by the soccer commentator Kenneth Wolstenholme - later to find fame as the man who exclaimed: 'some people are on the pitch. They think it's all over. It is now,' when England won the world cup in 1966 - who, as a schoolboy in Bolton, had seen Gus play in the 1930s. Although we do not have any sales figures, it must have been enough of a success for Stanley Paul to publish Lewis Jones's *King of Rugger* later in the same year.

How To Play Rugby League Football is a short guide to playing the game that appeared as part of a series of instructional books which included England cricketer and Arsenal footballer Denis Compton on *How To Play Association Football*, Jack Hobbs on *The Game of Cricket*, James Hartley on *How To Play Bowls Scientifically*, and many others. Gus explains the basics of the game with much common sense. The book's advice on passing, tackling and kicking remains as insightful as it was seventy years ago. Modern readers may be baffled by the importance placed on the scrum and the importance of dribbling for the forwards.

The rules of the game - which are reprinted at the end of the guide - also demonstrate just how much rugby league has changed.

The play-the-ball rule seems strange to us, with a three-yard rule in operation for all players in a ten-yard radius of the tackled player. Even stranger is the fact that a forward was allowed to hold the ball between his legs in the scrum and drive forward. This was a tactic that William Webb Ellis (wrongly credited by Gus as inventing rugby) would have recognised from the days when the game consisted of endless scrummaging at Rugby School, but it is doubtful whether it ever caught on among rugby league forwards. There is also much discussion of the mark and the fair catch, terms familiar to Australian Rules and American football fans respectively, but which haven't been part of league rules for half a century. But, as if to prove that there are few new things in the evolution of the game, the fair catch has reappeared today in the guise of defusing a bomb behind the goal-line. Most bizarre of all is the regulation against 'interference' by touch judges, presumably a throwback to the days when each club would contribute its own touch judge to the roster of match officials.

Rugby Renegade itself is a fascinating book. Most sporting biographies, then as much as now, are straightforward narratives of the highs and lows of the athlete's career. But Gus's book is remarkably modest and tends to gloss over many of the highlights of his playing career. It's difficult to get a sense of his towering reputation. Perhaps this is due in part to Kenneth Wolstenholme's lack of appreciation of Gus's greatness and standing in the game. But it is also because the book, in true rugby league fashion, also deals with the politics of rugby. Most of its chapters are actually about controversies in the game, whether it is rugby union hypocrisy or why the cup final should be played at Wembley. This is one of the reasons why the book remains so interesting. Gus is not bland and uncontroversial, as books of this nature often are, but determined to get his point over about what he feels is best for the sport.

There are, though, some wonderful moments of insight. Gus's description of the moment in the second half of the 1951 Championship Final when he realised that Workington had beaten Warrington ('it nearly made me swoon') or his memories of returning to Cumberland with the cup in 1950 are striking accounts. He also proves to be something of a prophet, predicting the emergence of a BBC2 Floodlit Trophy style competition and the move to two divisions. Twenty-first century readers coming to the book for the first time may also experience a sense of déjà vu. Gus debates whether the BBC are guilty of not giving the sport the publicity it deserves. And his assessment of the differences between league and union - 'league is a faster game, a much more intense and open game' - is one which has stood the test of time.

Reading *Rugby Renegade* one gets a sense that Gus took to rugby league so quickly as a teenager because it suited his temperament. He felt like an outsider, having been born to immigrant parents and brought up in the multi-racial melting pot of Cardiff's Tiger Bay. Interestingly, he attacks rugby union's treatment of rugby league as the equivalent of the 'colour bar', as discrimination against non-white people was known in 1950s Britain. The book's title is as much an affirmation of who he was as it is a mere description of his status. And like all those who are proud to be rugby league people, he turns the accusation that he is a renegade around to argue that it is not he who is in the wrong, but 'those who have insisted that that there should be two organisations' who are the real renegades, fostering intolerance and bitterness.

* * * * *

How did Gus compare to other truly great players? In 1988 he was one of the inaugural nine players to be inducted into the Rugby League Hall of Fame. Like Harold Wagstaff, Jim Sullivan, Brian Bevan and Alex Murphy, he would have been an automatic choice. In terms of games played and points scored, his record, to use the cliché, really did speak for itself. Changes in the way the game is played make comparisons between different generations almost impossible but, in the 1930s, there was really only one player who could be compared to Gus and that was Wigan's Jim Sullivan.

Gus and Jim were the binary stars of rugby league in their era. Although Sullivan was seven years older, they shared similar biographies, both being Welsh full-backs who became rugby league players at seventeen. Until Neil Fox eclipsed Sullivan's points scoring record, it was Sullivan and Gus who stood at the head of the all-time points scorers records. And while Sullivan played for just under twenty-five years, Gus played for just over a quarter of a century, although Sullivan played in more matches.

In the early 1930s it looked as if Gus would have a limited international career because of Jim Sullivan's absolute domination of the full-back position. Whenever Wigan played Salford there was always a bite in the air, as Salford carved a reputation as the Cherry and Whites' bogey team in the years before the war. It would have been easy for Gus to have been resentful, yet it is clear from *Rugby Renegade* that both players held each other in high regard. Their contrasting styles were sufficiently different that neither saw the other as a threat.

Sullivan was Rome to Risman's Greece. Sullivan was aggressive, driven and war-like. After the 1932 Battle of Brisbane, in which Great Britain were finally beaten by a ten-man Australian team in the bloodiest Test match of the inter-war period, Sullivan left the field raging at the loss, angrily telling his side after the match that if the game had gone on for five minutes more they could have won. His game was based not only on monumental skills but on physical intimidation. No-one who was tackled by Sullivan forgot it. Gus, in contrast, could be tough and uncompromising when necessary, especially in Test matches, but played a game based on artistry and creativity. His was a game of the finely-crafted pass, the imperceptible change of pace and the anticipation of an opponent's mistake. As well as a full-back, Gus was an all-time great centre and stand-off, but Sullivan commanded the full-back position like no-one before or since. Sullivan was the broadsword, Gus the rapier.

Introduction

* * * * *

When Gus Risman died at the age of eighty-three in 1994 it was just five days before Great Britain's twelve-man 8-4 victory over Australia, at Wembley. It was somehow appropriate that his death should be followed by an epic Ashes Test, just like so many in which he had been involved. But words like epic, monumental and incredible were always a feature of Gus Risman's career. It is the sheer scale of his achievements in rugby league that allow us to be so definite in our assessment of his genius. No-one will ever play the game for as long. It is very unlikely that anyone will ever score as many points as he did. And the nature of the game is such today that no-one will be able to build two or three separate careers in the way that Gus managed. His achievement is singular and will remain so.

Gus was no renegade. He was an athlete, an artist, a visionary and a leader of men. If anyone ever asks you why they call rugby league the greatest game of all, just tell them about Gus Risman.

Rugby Renegade

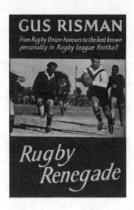

GUS RISMAN
From Rugby Union honours to the best known
personality in Rugby League football

Rugby Renegade

Original frontispiece (1958)

Rugby, they say, is the national sport of Wales; Rugby players the principal Welsh export.

Gus Risman has proved himself one of the greatest of those exports, great enough to be talked of still in Rugby Union circles, even though he became a renegade by joining the ranks of the Rugby League.

A player cast in the classical mould, Risman has thrilled Rugby crowds in Britain, Australia and New Zealand. He was a member of the all-conquering Salford side under the late Lance Todd, the Herbert Chapman of Rugby.

Risman has been equally successful as a manager, and when he took over the newly-formed Workington Town side he shocked the Rugby world by producing one of the game's strongest sides in incredibly short time.

Now manager of his old club, Salford, Gus Risman spices the story of his Rugby experiences with frank views on the never-ending, always discussed conflict between the two codes.

Knowing the faults and the strong points of each, he is not afraid to discuss either with equal force.

Rugby Renegade is an entertaining and provocative story, which will be read by all Rugby League fans - and by Rugby Union enthusiasts as well.

Rugby Renegade

1

THE BOY FROM TIGER BAY

The title of this book, *Rugby Renegade*, was only chosen in anticipation of what those narrow-minded characters who have worked so hard for the rugby split would say. Because I left my native South Wales and went North to play the Rugby League game, those staunch Rugby Union followers will call me a renegade, a traitor and one or two less printable words. They will refuse to understand or even listen to my point of view that there is just one game of rugby, and that the real renegades are those people who have insisted that there should be two organisations with slightly different sets of rules. For they are the people who have stunted the growth of the game in Britain. They are the people who have made certain that as far as the great mass of the general public is concerned, rugby is a localised sport.

All right, I can imagine the howls of protest that statement will cause, but just consider the facts. Rugby League is confined to the three northern counties of Lancashire, Yorkshire and Cumberland. It is, I know, played

Rugby Renegade

in Australia, New Zealand and in France, but for the moment we are just considering the position at home.

Rugby Union is played, admittedly, all over Britain, but in very few areas can it be regarded as a really major sport. Public interest is rarely great, and there is hardly a soul in the border country of Scotland who could tell you how Cardiff are doing in any particular season, or even which players are in the Cardiff team. Only when the internationals come around does the interest become widespread, and even then we have to admit that a big soccer game, say between Manchester United and Tottenham Hotspur, will arouse more public interest and occupy more newspaper space than the clash of two countries at Twickenham, Arms Park, Lansdowne Road or Murrayfield.

And all because of intolerance. All because too many people have littered the game with bitterness and steadfastly refused to forget old quarrels.

Many people in Wales refuse to recognise the right of any man to capitalise his talents. To hear them talk you would think that as young Augustus John Risman played in the streets of Tiger Bay, Cardiff, he was dreaming of turning professional.

Yes, like Billy Boston, a great rugby player if ever I saw one, and Shirley Bassey and Joe Erskine, I am a product of that wonderful area of Cardiff called Tiger Bay. It is a wonderful area because for years people of every nationality, colour, race and religion have lived, worked and played there without a hint of intolerance or bitterness. A spot of the Tiger Bay spirit might well have been the making of this game of rugby.

Father kept a boarding house for seamen in the area, and along with the rest of the kids there I had to make my own fun. At South Church Street School, Cardiff, there were no organised games for us youngsters, so we arranged our own games in the streets and on the spare bits of rough land. We would play rugby, using old magazines or pigs' bladders as the ball. It was under conditions like this that I learned the basic arts of rugby. You have to have a safe pair of hands to catch a pig's bladder or a pile of magazines tied together with string, and you had to make your sidesteps perfectly in the cramped space of a Canal Parade or Sophia Street. All the same, we learned fast, and we even discovered the 'art' of drop-kicking these improvised balls! Many was the time later on in my career when I took a drop-kick at goal and thanked my early training in the back streets of Tiger Bay.

We kids were rugby daft in those days, and when we weren't playing our own particular type of rugby we were watching the local club, Loudouns. We were their staunchest supporters.

But in 1922 my father left Cardiff and moved to Barry, where he kept two cafes, one on the sea-front and one in the town. This meant a change of school for me and I waved goodbye to South Church Street School and said hello to Gladstone Road School, Barry.

I was eleven in those days - I was born on March 21, 1911 - and just behind me in the school was a boy called George Green. He was later to play soccer for Charlton Athletic and Wales. There was also another lad at Gladstone Road whom I shall never forget. He was tiny and chubby, and instead of kicking a football or tennis ball or rag ball around as most of the other lads did, he would turn up in the school yard swinging a putter. I cannot remember ever seeing him without it - he probably took it to bed with him! Every spare moment he had he would spend swinging his putter, or - and this was when he was really lucky - would take out an old golf ball and carefully stroke it with the precious club.

No doubt that incessant practice has helped my old school chum a lot in later life. For after all, Dai Rees hasn't done too badly in the golf world, has he? His father, by the way, was pro at the local Brynhill Golf Club.

Gladstone School was a soccer school and during my three years there I never gave rugby a thought. Soccer was my game, and I took to it like a duck to water. How I loved my soccer! I got into the school team, then into the town team and at the age of thirteen I had a Welsh schoolboys' international trial.

So great was my love for soccer that every day my ambition to become a soccer star grew stronger. I played whenever I could, except on Saturday afternoons, when, along with my pals, I would go on the bus from Barry to Cardiff to watch the great Cardiff City side of those days. The fare was a penny, which was a fortune back then, so we lads often used to scrounge a ride on the bus for nothing, and I must owe the Cardiff City club quite a lot of money for the number of times I have slipped into Ninian Park without paying!

True we used to watch a bit of rugby at Cardiff Arms Park or at Barry when Cardiff City were away from home, but our great heroes in those days were such Ninian Park stars as Jimmy Blair, Bill Hardy and Fred Keenor.

After three years at Gladstone Road I won a scholarship to the Barry County School (it is now called Barry Grammar School). This not only meant a change of school but also a change of sports, for the County School played rugby, not soccer. And what fine rugby players it turned out, too, for among my contemporaries were Ronnie Boon and Danny Evans, both of whom went on to win caps for Wales.

The change didn't worry me. All I wanted to do was to play football, and I didn't really care whether it was soccer or rugby. I played for the school both as a junior and as a senior. We played other grammar schools in the area, but there were no town and county representative matches as there were for the soccer schools. The highest honour possible was to represent Wales in their one match against Yorkshire secondary schools. I only managed to get into one of the trials.

We played our rugby matches at school on Saturday mornings, and in the afternoon I would play soccer for Barry West End, a local team. I had formed no strong preference for either game - I loved them both - and I haven't changed as I have got older. I still enjoy watching both games and, until I got too old to play, I would quite willingly have played soccer as well as rugger.

Not all boys are like that, though, which is why schools, grammar schools in particular, should cater for both rugby and soccer. It is unfair that the boys should have to play the game the headmaster prefers, for a lad with a natural bent towards soccer will find his sporting life miserable at a rugby school. In this way we can well lose many would-be soccer players.

I know that schools claim that they have not the facilities to provide for both sports. Playing-field accommodation is limited, and the coaching has to be done by the teaching staff, and it might be impossible to find enough teachers to give the boys coaching in both soccer and rugby.

But these are just excuses. There are many admirable courses which schoolmasters can take to fit themselves for coaching duties, and the question of playing-fields and finance would not have arisen if successive Governments had not spent their time taking money out of sport instead of helping it.

Future champion sportsmen and women are made in the schools. If a boy or a girl gets a good grounding, half the battle is won, and would take the merest fraction out of the national budget to provide schools with the necessary facilities for a proper sporting education. That money need not come out of general taxation. The Government takes a very hefty slice of the income of the football pools, so is it too much to expect that some of that money be used to provide our schools with enough facilities for the boys and girls to take part in soccer, rugby, cricket, tennis, swimming and athletics? After all, sport has paid so much in Entertainments Tax, which lasted as 'an emergency measure' from the First World War until 1957, that it has a right to expect the Government to add a bit of give to its take.

It is fatuous to have modern grammar schools without adequate accommodation for sport. Yet how many of our grammar schools have enough soccer pitches, rugby pitches, cricket pitches, and tennis courts, not to mention an athletics track or a swimming-pool?

It is incredible that we have made such magnificent strides in swimming yet we have only two indoor swimming-baths in Britain which are the required international length - Brighton, and the Derby Baths at Blackpool! Barry has one over a hundred yards long, but it is an outdoor pool. What a shocking state of affairs for an allegedly sporting nation!

In the city where I lived - Salford, in Lancashire - they have just built a new boys' grammar school. Goodness knows it was needed, because the old one had entered the ancient class. It is a lovely modern school, but the plan to give it its own swimming-pool was turned down as too expensive.

Too expensive for the only boys' grammar school in the city! And the Government has spent years taking money out of sport by way of Entertainment Tax and Pools Tax.

It could happen in no other country, and the way we behave, the encouragement we give to our youngsters, we don't deserve even the hint of success in any sport.

2

ECONOMICS TAKE CHARGE

My turn for leaving school came at the end of the Christmas term, 1928. I was then seventeen-and-a-half years of age. I had received a good education, and I had won the School Certificate. It was therefore reasonable to expect that I would be able to get into a job with some prospects of advancement.

But Christmas, 1928, is a date which strikes terror into the hearts of many people who lived in the industrial areas, and South Wales was no exception. In fact South Wales could well claim to be one of the most affected areas. Yes, it was that dreaded word 'depression'.

The great slump was under way and it was increasing in severity. A seventeen-and-a-half-year-old boy, even with the School Certificate, was just another number on the labour market, just another man looking for a job, just another man for whom no work could be found.

Grown men were willing to take on the most menial task, but there were not even any vacancies on the register of menial tasks. I tramped from factory to factory, from shop to shop, from office to office. But it was no good. There were no jobs for skilled men, let alone for boys just out of school.

Those days will never be forgotten in South Wales. Many people today try to kid themselves that the depression never existed, that it was just a bad dream. But exist it did, and the fertile industrial area of South Wales rapidly rotted until its cities, its towns, its villages, its works and its people almost ceased to exist.

I applied for more than fifty jobs, but always it was the same answer...'No.' I tried to get any sort of work, but there were even a dozen men waiting to take over a job as a road sweeper.

What this idleness did to grown men, many of whom were skilled workers, I shudder to think, but I do know that it almost drove me mad. Times were hard at home because Father had diabetes, and all the family's money was spent on treating him. I wanted to help by adding something to the flimsy family budget, but there was no work in South Wales.

Eventually I struck lucky and got a job on a boat as a messroom boy. Many were the envious eyes that were turned towards me when it was known that I had got work. Even skilled engineers or experienced coal-miners would have been glad to take on my job.

My first trip was from Barry to Liverpool, and at Liverpool the world crashed around me....the boat was sold. I was paid off with the rest of the crew, and all I received for the fourteen-day trip was two pounds (a handsome reward in those hard times) and my railway fare back home.

I was out of work again.

Despite the seriousness of the depression, sport went on. After all, men had to do something, and one way to take a man's mind off the hard times was to provide sport in the shape of rugby and soccer.

I joined the rugby club at Dinas Powis, which is a small town between Cardiff and Barry. We had to pay all our expenses with Dinas Powis, so when Cardiff Scottish asked me to turn out for them I jumped at the chance. After all, Cardiff Scottish paid all the expenses of their players!

My first game for Cardiff Scottish was at Stroud, in Gloucestershire, and just before the match a man called Frank Young, who represented many Rugby League teams in the South Wales area, stopped me in the street and asked me what I thought about Rugby League.

I was shocked! To talk about Rugby League was a sin comparable with blasphemy in the chapel. In the public-house, which served as the changing-room at Stroud, there were notices which warned us of dire penalties if we even so much as talked to a Rugby League scout, and we youngsters were left in no doubt that serious as theft and murder may be, the greatest crime of all was to let the words 'Rugby League' pass our lips, or thoughts of the game enter our minds.

I didn't play at all well at Stroud, but on my return home Mr. Young got in touch with me again. He told me that he would try to fix up a trial for me with Leeds, and it began to dawn on me that maybe it was not all that criminal to think of becoming a Rugby League player.

Though it was impossible to get work in South Wales, it still cost money to live. The depression was getting worse and worse and even if the industrial health of the country did improve quickly, it was perfectly obvious that it would be some time before all the scars were healed, before there was work for all of us.

The Rugby League clubs were, at least, offering some money, and no one in South Wales could afford to ignore the offer of money in those desperate days. It is all very well people sitting back comfortably and talking of amateurism, but a man, even a youngster under the age of eighteen, has to live and eat. The chance of playing Rugby League football for money was as glittering a prospect to me in those days as a Treble Chance win to most people today.

So I told Mr. Young I was interested in his offers, and when he got into touch with me again he told me that he had arranged for me to have a trial with the Salford club. Apparently Leeds were not interested.

Everything had to be kept quiet, otherwise I should have been hounded out of the Rugby Union game just for listening to Mr.Young's overtures. Not even my people must know what was going on, so I told them I was leaving Wales and going to England in search of work. So many other people were doing the same thing that no one thought to question my statement.

Naturally, I dare not allow anyone to know where I was staying - the scouts of Rugby Union spread their net widely, even after unknown seventeen-and-a-half-year-olds - so it was impossible for anyone to get in touch with me. But for that my career might have developed along very different lines.

For, like every youngster in and around Cardiff, I cherished an ambition to play rugby for Cardiff and eventually for Wales. Cardiff Arms Park was like sacred ground to us all. And it was while I was away in Salford that a letter arrived at my home. It invited me to turn out for the Cardiff 'B' team.

Here, then, was a strange situation. Cardiff were inviting me to play for them - true, only in the 'B' team, but it was still Cardiff - and I was longing to play for the team I, and many others, called The Rugby team.

Yet I was away in the North, so the letter of invitation just lay unopened on the table!

That was how I lost the opportunity of achieving my

ambition to play on Cardiff Arms Park. I had been on the ground many times as a spectator, but I had never played there... and a move to Rugby League would mean that I never would play there.

During my time at Gladstone Road School I had run on Arms Park in a relay race and I still have a gold medal for that race. I cherish it not for the fact that we won the race but because the medal was won on Cardiff Arms Park.

It is a little ironical that my change to Rugby League barred me from playing on Arms Park, yet when I did eventually achieve my ambition and play there it was as a professional League player. It was during the war, when the Union-League war was suspended in favour of the much more important conflict, and I played in a representative team alongside Union men.

So if I had not left home and gone to Salford for a trial I might well have made my name as a Union player. But I also missed another chance through my disappearance.

During the month I was in Salford, the secretary of the Barry West End soccer team was searching everywhere for me. It appears that Tottenham Hotspur had heard about my success on the soccer field and they were anxious for me to go to White Hart Lane for a trial. So who knows, if I hadn't gone to Salford for a trial as a Rugby League player I might well have joined Tottenham Hotspur as a soccer player.

And I would have enjoyed that just as much.

But one cannot live on 'if's and 'buts'..... especially in the middle of a depression!

I didn't, of course, sign professional for Salford immediately. I had a month's trial as an amateur, and frankly I didn't do too well. I found a lot of differences in the Rugby League game and it was difficult trying to make the grade. However, the club asked me to come back for another month, and it was in the first match of that second months' trial that I broke my ankle. Fortunately, it was only a chipped bone and I was only out of the game for four weeks.

I came back for the very last match of the 1929 season and was chosen to play for Salford 'A' team against Leigh 'A' team, and I don't mind admitting that I was frightened at the thought of going out to face those big fellows.

Immediately opposite me was a former international player, Walter Mooney, and almost the first time I got the ball he came for me. Without thinking, I stuck out my hand just at the right moment and handed him off perfectly. This created an opening and we scored a try, and that one move gave me back all my confidence.

Nevertheless, I was still dubious about turning professional. I was not certain that I had either the skill or the physique, and to this very day I believe that no boy should be allowed to go into senior football until he has reached the age of eighteen. So much can happen when a lad is immature, and for every young star who develops early there are a lot of young players who are ruined. One really bad shaking-up can knock all the confidence out of a boy, and any lad who is not big and tough can have his career ruined and the game can lose a possible star. After all, a really tough, but fair, tackle can shake the best of men, so the effect on a young boy is frightening.

At the time I was on trial with Salford the club was managed by the greatest manager of all time, Lance Todd. It was Mr. Todd who saw to it that I was put in digs, played in the 'A' team and was given the fantastic amount of five shillings a week pocket money - that, to a boy from South Wales in the early part of 1929, was a fortune.

Mr. Todd found me a job as a junior clerk at the end of the season and I felt the happiest lad alive - I had a job. I had wanted work more than anything else, and here I was with a job. What a great thrill it was!

But it was a temporary job that only lasted for a month, and then back home I went to Barry not knowing whether I had made the grade or not. But I trained on the beach and on Barry Island's Spion Kop. Many times I wrote to Mr. Todd during that summer, and I couldn't help worrying as the weeks went by and there was no word from the club.

Then it came, just about a week before the start of the new season I was asked to report for training, and when I arrived in Salford I was offered professional terms. The offer was a signing-on fee of £52 paid over the following year at a pound a week. It was a tremendous sum for a youngster in those days, but at the time Father was very ill and we desperately needed money. I told this to Mr. Todd and, as was so typical of the man, he gave me another £25 in cash.

I was also found a job as a junior clerk at the Shell-Mex Offices in Manchester. My pay for playing rugby was £3 if we won, thirty-five shillings if we lost. And it was a case of no play, no pay.

My debut in the first team came in the very first match of the season. It was against Barrow at The Willows, the home of the Salford club, and I was chosen on the right wing, a position in which I had never played before in my life. We were 0-10 at half-time and I wasn't very happy in my unaccustomed position. Then in the second half, Charlie Carr, the Barrow centre who had just returned from a tour with the Great Britain side, threw out a pass which I intercepted. I raced away as fast as I could and touched down between the posts for our first try of the season.

Even that didn't make my performance a good one, and I was quite hurt by some of the remarks of the crowd, who kept telling me where to go!

Our second match was an away game against St. Helens Recs, and when the team sheet was posted on the notice-

Rugby Renegade

board I saw that Llew Williams, our full-back, had been
dropped and I was to take his place.

I took to full-back like a duck to water. A full-back has
room to move and time to think, and as kicking was one of
my strong points I was much happier than I had been on the
wing.

In fact, I never looked back after that move to full-back.

3

THE UNION MAN HAS A LOT TO LEARN

Like every other player who graduates from Union to League, I had a lot to learn when I signed for Salford. For no matter how good a Union player is, it will take him some time before he can fit into a League side.

His first worry will be the difference in the constitution of a League side from a Union side, and the slight difference in rules. In Rugby Union there are fifteen players to each side, with eight of them comprising the forwards. In Rugby League two of those forwards are dropped and each side is made up of thirteen players.

Once a player has got used to that - and it should not take him long - he has to get it firmly into his head that there are certain fundamental differences in the laws of the two codes. In Union you have only to kick the ball into touch to be happy, but in the League game it is necessary for the ball to bounce before it goes into touch. If it goes into touch after a bounce, the scrum is formed at a point opposite where the ball crossed the touchline. But if the ball did not bounce before going into touch, then it is what we call a 'ball back', and the scrum is formed on the point from which the ball was kicked.

Many Union players have fallen down on this when they have changed to the League game. It is so easy to find touch safely in Union that the players will kick their way out of trouble. As soon as they are in danger of being tackled they will kick, and even if only about ten yards are gained, it is still regarded as a good kick.

But in Rugby League you have to kick more carefully and you cannot clutch at the straw of a big punt into the stands. True, no one can claim that it is possible to judge the bounce of a rugby ball after a kick, so no one can claim that the Rugby League rule calls for more accurate kicking. But what it does call for is longer kicking, when kicking is necessary, and it also means that a kick is a last resort. After all, rugby is essentially a handling game. Players have to play their way out of trouble instead of kicking the ball into the stands.

The other great difference a Union man will find when he takes up the League game is that when he is tackled he must not release the ball as he does in Rugby Union. A tackle stops a Rugby League game, and the tackled player must be allowed to get to his feet and 'play the ball', usually with a back-heel to one of his colleagues.

Even the mathematics of the two codes is different. In Rugby League all goals count as two points, whereas in Rugby Union a penalty goal or drop goal counts as three points. Then even the score-lines are given differently. When a Rugby Union side has scored a goal it means that a try has been converted and the side has scored five points, but in Rugby League a converted try is shown as one goal one try, equalling, of course, the same number of points.

But those are just the academic differences, and any intelligent man can get used to them in no time at all. There are, however, much more important differences, which explain why many a Rugby Union player takes some time to settle down to the League game. In fact it might be true to say that only the really star Union player - the international - could hold down his place in a League side right from the very start.

For Rugby League is much more intense than Rugby Union. That doesn't mean it is a dirtier or a rougher game, but simply that there is a lot more action and that the players are in the thick of the game much more. The ball moves about much more quickly than it does in Union, probably due to the fact that with four fewer men on the field the players have to sustain their efforts for longer periods.

There is not nearly the same amount of kicking in League as in Union, no doubt due to the fact that it is not as easy to find touch safely, and the players are expected to cover more ground, keep more in the game and handle the ball more.

So only the exceptionally good footballer can make the change successfully without a three-month 'acclimatising' period in which life is very hard indeed. Training schedules in the League are much more severe because we expect our players to work harder than they are expected to do in Rugby Union. The game itself is a faster one, and Rugby League players do more work and see far more of the game than do their opposite numbers in Rugby Union.

For instance, it is quite possible for a Rugby Union forward to go through the whole eighty minutes of a game without handling the ball. That is not to say that he is hiding himself, but the forward play in Union is vastly different from the forward play in League. The Union forwards push and shove in the loose and set scrums and they take part in the dribbling runs. But they are not really expected to make sensational runs with the ball in their hands. That is the work of the three-quarters.

Rugby Renegade

In Rugby League this just would not work. No forward is ever able to go through a game without handling the ball. If he did he would soon find himself out of the side. For we expect our big, burly forwards to play the part of three-quarters. We expect them to be able to pick up the ball and make runs of forty or fifty yards. Yes, we even expect that of hookers and the other two front-row men. There is no place in a Rugby League side for the man who cannot run with the ball ... and when he is running he has got to run fast, because speed is all-important.

Some people believe that the tactical moves in the two codes are dissimilar, but they are not. Pretty much the same sort of moves will succeed in both, with the exception that kicking is not nearly so effective in League as in Union. That is the first lesson we have to teach any player when he first signs for a Rugby League club - do not kick at each and every opportunity. A kick in Rugby League is only permissible if it will gain a lot of ground by finding touch or if it is a through kick or a cross-field kick which will allow a colleague to streak through a gap in the defence.

But although the tactics are pretty much the same, the correct execution of them is of greater importance in the League game. There is not the same sense of urgency in Rugby Union, nor the same sort of worry if a particular move breaks down. In Union it is just one of those things, but in League it is vitally important that every man realises where and how a certain move broke down, and that he is determined that there will be no repeat mistakes.

Unlike the League player, the Union man has not the worry of shaping his tactics to produce a fast-moving, open game because no one worries overmuch if a Union match is not open. The spectators have not really come to see rugby as a spectacle. They have come to cheer on their own side, and if the players enjoy the game everyone is happy.

In Rugby League it is different. We have paying customers to entertain, and these paying customers demand open football. They want to see the three-quarters getting the ball and flinging it about, and if they don't see that they jolly well want to know the reason why. As a result we expect our forwards to be extremely versatile, to be able to pick up the ball, run with it at speed and join the three-quarters in a passing movement.

So Rugby League is a faster game, a much more intense and open game, in which every one of the twenty-six players takes a more active part than in Rugby Union.

That is why it takes some time for a Rugby Union player to get accustomed to the Northern code. But no Rugby Union player need worry....the first three months are the worst, as I found out.

Rugby Renegade

4

THIS SILLY WAR

Although there are differences in the rules and differences in the technique between Rugby League and Rugby Union, it is only right to remember that both games are games of rugby. Any player should in my view be able to change from one to the other after a three months' trial period, for the basic principles are the same in both games.

But the Rugby League and the Rugby Union have split, and today the wound is as deep as it ever was. Other sports have peace between their amateurs and professionals, but in rugby there appears to be incessant friction.

The split took place many, many years ago, and the reasons for the split were exactly the same as those for the split in association football - professionalism. All sport in Britain used to be on an amateur basis, and then, in rugby as in soccer, the industrial workers in the North realised that they could pick up a few shillings broken time pay for playing their football, and as times were hard in those days they saw no reason why they shouldn't do so.

Rugby Renegade

This meant the introduction of professionalism, which was something that certain people could not stand. As a result there was a split, and the Northern Union (the Rugby League) was formed.

The same split occurred in soccer, but in soccer there were apparently more people with good sense than there were in rugby. Differences were patched up so that today soccer lives in peace. The Football Association controls the sport - both amateur and professional - and the game has prospered in consequence. Amateurs and professionals can play side by side in the same teams, and amateurs have even won full international honours for England. Amateur teams even take part in the F.A. Cup, Britain's premier sporting competition.

But in rugby? Not on your life! Once a man turns professional he is finished for all time with the Rugby Union game and code. He doesn't even need to turn professional. He need only have a trial game with a Rugby League club and he becomes to all intents and purposes a professional player.

Just think of it. A lad comes along to me at Salford and asks for a trial. If he so much as kicks a ball with any of my professional players he will be barred for life from Rugby Union - yes, even if he fails to make the grade in the trial and never actually signs professional forms. Could you get more dogmatic and short-sighted than that?

Why, the player need not even kick a ball for a Rugby League team. He need only think about it. One Welsh player I know was once on his way to play for his country when it became known that he had spoken to a Rugby League contact. He had come to no agreement with the League side, and it could be that he might never have signed professional. But he had been in verbal contact with the Rugby League and that was enough. He was taken off the train immediately and his place in the national side was given to another player. Yes, the man was dropped from an international side on the way to the game just because he had spoken to a Rugby League contact!

No wonder the player eventually turned professional. There was no future for him in the Union game.

Yet such Union stalwarts cannot even be consistent. When lads go into one of the Services they can play football with and against each other irrespective of the fact that some of the lads are professionals. During the war, the finest Union sides contained many professional Rugby League men.

I had the honour of skippering the Army side and the Welsh international side during the war. In our team were some of the most famous of Union stars like Haydn Tanner, Bleddyn Williams, Wendy Davis and Wilf Wooller. But we also had Emlyn Jenkins, Alan Edwards, Trevor Foster, Doug Phillips and other professional League men. It was all right for us to join forces then. But not now.

You might think that inconsistent, but inconsistency is not uncommon in this context. Rugby League touring sides visit this country from Australia and New Zealand and make their headquarters at Ilkley in Yorkshire. Naturally, they want to have a ground on which they can train and practice, but do you think the Ilkley Rugby Union club is allowed to put its facilities at the disposal of our visitors from the Commonwealth as it would like to do? Not on your life! That would never do! Our own cousins, who shower us with hospitality when any of our sporting teams visit their countries, are snubbed.

Yet, Bob Scott, the famous All Blacks' full-back, is feted when he visits this country with a Rugby Union team ... and Bob Scott has openly admitted that from 1936 until 1941 he played Rugby League. Without knowing it, the Rugby Union have feted an ex-Rugby League man!

But the Rugby Union will use the Rugby League when it suits its purpose. It did during the war. It has done since. For when the Australian Rugby Union touring side met a combined Lancashire & Cheshire XV a few years ago it was decided that there was not a Rugby Union ground big enough to hold the crowd which wanted to attend. And who do you think normally played at Belle Vue? Why, none other than the Belle Vue Rangers Rugby League team!

Another big representative Rugby Union game in Manchester was recently played at Maine Road, Manchester, which is the home of the Manchester City Association Football Club - a professional club. But maybe the Rugby Union thinks that a soccer professional is not quite so bad as a Rugby League one!

Strangely enough, though, the Union people who say that Rugby League is a professional game are not correct. It would be more correct to say the Rugby League allows professionalism. But there are more amateurs playing Rugby League than there are professionals, for in Lancashire, Yorkshire and Cumberland, which is the Rugby League territory, there are scores of junior amateur sides.

The junior sides are producing a steady flow of senior recruits to the game - other junior players, like such players in other sports, have no desire to turn professional. However, this flow is not sufficient, and there is always a market for the top class Rugby Union man in the League game. And there are, I believe, some Rugby Union men willing to pocket money from a professional League club as 'scout's commission'.

In fact it is now much easier to sign Union players than it was in the old days. At one time Rugby League representatives in Wales had to run the risk of being thrown into the local river. But not any longer.

Now we don't have to send men from the North. Instead

we get regular reports from Rugby Union people who are only too willing to act as our representatives!

In addition to the players who are recommended by our scouts, we get a steady stream of Rugby Union players who approach us direct and ask for trials. They come from all over Britain, and some of them are well-known players. They play under assumed names and then go back to their Rugby Union game if they are not offered professional terms.

Other Union players often ask our help in training, and the Salford club is always open to any Rugby Union player who wishes to have a training spin or some massage. These players are never asked to sign forms. We just place our facilities at their disposal if they wish to come along - many ring us up to ask for those facilities - purely and simply because they are rugby players, and in my view a player is a rugby player whether he plays for fun or for money. We never ask Rugby Union players to visit us. They ask us. And we would never refuse help to any sportsman - rugby player, soccer player, athlete, cricketer, tennis player or anything else.

The Rugby Union may possibly disagree with our attitude, but so far as I am concerned that is the principle we adopt.

But back to the signing of Union players. Those who do not approach the League clubs are recommended by scouts, who may be Union men. They are watched in their Union games, and then, if the report is a good one, the League club itself sends a representative. Many is the time I have been on Union grounds and watched players, although officially the Rugby Union does not, I believe, allow League men admission to their grounds!

The first approach to a player is not hard these days, and it is amazing how many people are only too anxious to help in making appointments. Sometimes there is trouble from a player's family, and many is the time that family ties have stopped a signing right at the last minute. On one occasion a player's father was very much against his son signing. He brushed aside all the promises, pointing out that 'money talks'.

It did, in the shape of five hundred one-pound notes as a first installment on the transfer fee!

But these cash-only deals are a rarity. Such tactics are only employed in the direst emergency. Usually cheques are good enough!

Most Rugby Union players take it as a compliment when they are noticed and approached by a Rugby League club. Many of them have been known to complain when an approach does not materialise. They think then that they are not worth considering, and no player likes to think that.

If the Rugby League approach does not come quickly enough, one or two such players are not against making their own approach. They just write, telephone or call and ask for a trial. There are many cases of this on record with almost every Rugby League club. One club, in fact, received a letter signed by a couple of Rugby Union players, both of whom wanted a trial. The club agreed... and was shocked to find that a party of ten turned up. The party included the players, the agent, advisers and members of the respective families!

It is not always so easy to get a player on trial, though. Many Rugby Union players have extremely good jobs and they cannot see the advantages of turning professional. The only way these players can be persuaded is by the offer of a similar job in the North and also by the payment of a very generous signing-on fee. Unfortunately, the fees paid to some of the Rugby Union stars have been so high that many less capable Union players have received an exaggerated idea of their own ability. They, too, ask for tremendous signing-on fees when they are, quite frankly, not worth it.

Another deterrent to a Union player throwing in his lot with the Rugby League is the punishment that can be meted out by the Rugby Union authorities. Once a League form has been signed there is no going back. The player has made himself an outcast for the rest of his life.

I am sure that many players would be only too glad to have their old colleagues back in the fold, but some among the officials who administrate the game will not hear of it. So great is the power of these people that more than one well-known Union player has told me he is scared to death of being seen talking to any League player or official - even to one of his old team-mates. Such fraternisation could easily cost a Rugby Union player his county or international cap.

What utter nonsense it is, and how glad I am that many Rugby Union players go out of their way to flout this ridiculous and unsporting position. However, many of the professional players when they go back home are reluctant to seek out old acquaintances because of the penalties they know that the Rugby Union game can inflict.

Yet many former Rugby League players go back to their home towns and have the greatest desire to settle down into their old way of life and help the local club. To debar them is stupid. Many of them have won international honours and nearly all have served the game of rugby faithfully and well as good sportsmen. Why, then, should they be blacklisted?

But blacklisted they are, and I believe that some players who turned professional after winning Union international honours have even been refused their Union international caps.

How mean can you get?

But then these returned professionals are rarely, if ever,

forgiven. They are not allowed to join their local club as social members. They are certainly not allowed to coach any of the youngsters. They cannot even go into the club-house for a drink.

One former Rugby League player got round that rather severe rule by joining the bowls section of his local Rugby Union club. He was having a drink at the bar one night when he was told by one of the officials to leave. He calmly produced his membership card... and offered the rugby official a drink!

Fortunately, a number of clubs are enlightened enough to ignore this particular type of 'colour' bar. I say: 'More power to their arm!'.

What talent the Rugby Union world throws away by this nonsense! In other sports they are only too anxious to use former players as coaches. Even lawn tennis, where the amateurism complex - or should it be the shamateurism complex? - is extremely strong, allows its junior players to be coached by professionals. Cricket, soccer and other sports all allow former professional players to coach juniors, thereby raising the standard of play in all grades. Why, then, will not rugby allow the same sort of facilities to its players?

Actually, we see inconsistency raising its mighty head once again, for there are cases of professionals coaching juniors and Rugby Union clubs. George Bennett, of Wigan, and George Brown, of Leeds, coached Rugby Union clubs for many years. I have coached Rugby Union schoolboys. So have other professional Rugby League players. Why, then, can't this state of affairs be recognised and such freedom allowed as general rule? Why can't former League players be accepted for what they are - just plain, ordinary fellows who have played the game of rugby professionally?

There is nothing disgraceful about being a professional. Nobody despises the man who capitalises his talents as a writer (as many former R.U. players have), as a doctor, as a lawyer or as a singer. Why, then, should anyone despise a man who capitalises his talents as a sporting performer?

After all, it is far better for a man to say openly 'I am a professional and, although I love the game as deeply as any amateur, I am going to capitalise my talents and take money for playing', than it is for a man to say 'I am going to be regarded as an amateur, but nobody is going to know what I get on the side'.

We all know the stories about the difference between a top-class professional being five pounds a week - on the side of the amateur - or that a professional pays income tax on his earnings whereas an amateur doesn't. Unfortunately, to some extent those sayings are true. In most top-class amateur sport there is this deadly disease to contend with. We get it in show jumping, we get it in athletics, we get it in soccer - and we get it at times in rugby.

This kind of thing in Rugby Union is now far from uncommon, so that sometimes when a player signs a professional form and joins a Rugby League club he is only legalising his status!

Once upon a time the story went that a number of amateur players received their 'perquisites' in the toe of their shoes. They would find a few pound notes carefully rolled up, and it was a strict rule that no one tried to find out who had left the little gift. Now, so rumour has it, some amateurs are more refined, and some players are handed the money in packets.

The easy way to arrange this kind of thing is, or course, by expenses. I know how it is done because I have done it. During the war when I played for Wales at Rugby Union I travelled from Aldershot. I told the officials that my expenses were £4. That, admittedly, was allowing for one or two 'extras' which nobody can work out when travelling. In other words, I was making a few shillings profit. My heart stopped when the officials told me that my expenses couldn't be right. But my heart started beating again when I was handed £8!

Another Rugby League player travelled long distances to play in these matches, and he admits that he supplemented his Army pay by the amount he 'made' on the expenses offered to him. He admits to liking the 'rates of pay' given to such amateurs.

These amateurs can easily 'justify' their expenses. Taxi fares are allowed when, perhaps, train or bus has been used. Liberal meal allowances are given. And there is a general allowance for sundries. I know, because I have received them as an amateur.

But this kind of amateur can get other perquisites. Many of them are also given free equipment and allowed laundry and maintenance expenses. Some clubs lay on free lunches, dinners and drinks, and pleasant tours are paid for by the club. The players don't pay a penny. Even their haircuts, cigarettes and drinks are put on the club's bill at the hotels!

Is this the great spirit of amateurism?

You could, I suppose, make a case to justify these liberal expenses, but it would seem that some star Union players are almost receiving what amounts to a living wage from their amateur clubs. Some, I am told, are getting as much for playing Rugby Union as an amateur as they would for playing Rugby League as a professional.

The possible rewards open to a star Rugby Union man need not end here. Players are sometimes found good jobs with excellent prospects. Others have presents given to their wives or families.

More than one big deal, with a Rugby Union star being on the verge of turning professional, has been stopped at the last minute by the arrival of a lucrative offer. Even offers of £4,000 by Rugby League clubs have been turned down.

Now how can a man turn down an offer of £4,000, plus payment for playing football, plus a well-paid job and often a house at a ludicrously low rent? Remember these offers make a Rugby Union star capable of earning much more than the most highly paid soccer star if he will only turn professional.

But often these offers are refused. And why? Simply because the unofficial inducement to stay in Rugby Union has been even greater than the offer from Rugby League. It has perhaps been made worth the player's while financially to remain an amateur. He might even find that he will get an excellent job - sometimes even put in line for a directorship - and his 'expenses' increased to a very liberal figure that the mere professionals cannot match. The player who says he stays in Rugby Union for the love of the game and camaraderie therein can be commended, but you can be sure he is financially secure, or has a reasonably good job.

All these things go on. There is a boy playing Rugby League today who had the shock of his life when he played his first senior Rugby Union game. He travelled about a mile and a half to the ground for the game... and then discovered that he was given £3 for his expenses. This afterwards became a regular payment. Just think of it, £3 a week for a youngster just out of junior football!

That is the way things are done in a number of cases, and yet the out-and-out honest professional is often ostracised by those who think they are administering a completely amateur sport! We are not supposed to be good enough to mix with them, any player who so much as has a trial with us (and gets found out!) is banished from the game.

What a pity it all is. There is just one game of rugby, and even though we have two different ways of playing it, there is no reason why the two codes should not live in peace with each other. There is no reason why the Rugby Union player who thinks he is good enough should not be allowed to have a trial with a League team and then go back to Union if it is found that he will not make the grade. There is no reason why a professional, once he has finished playing, should not be able to join his local Rugby Union club if he wants to and become one of its supporters.

Far better for us to live in peace and work together for the good of rugby as a whole than to be glaring at each other from opposite sides of the fence when everyone knows what is going on.

This much, however, I will say. I have never found any animosity existing between the players of the two codes. In the Rugby League areas you find the players meeting away from their clubs, and you find Rugby Union players, when they have no match, sitting in the stand or standing on the terraces cheering on their local Rugby League side. They are just rugby players cheering on rugby players.

The trouble lies with some people with long memories who can never forgive the Northern people for the break and for the formation of the Rugby League, which allowed open professionalism as opposed to amateurism that is sometimes open to question.

All I can say to that is that there was a split, just as serious and just as severe, in soccer. Tempers and passions ran just as high. But the soccer people buried the hatchet and the game has prospered, both for the amateurs and for the professionals.

Why should the same thing not happen in rugby?

5

SELLING OURSELVES

We of Rugby League must face the facts. It is no use kidding ourselves that ours is a major sport because it is not. The Rugby League game in Britain has made little or no progress over the years, and it is still confined to Lancashire, Yorkshire and Cumberland. The only successful missionary work that has been done has taken place in Cumberland, where no senior side existed until after World War II.

Against the success in Cumberland we must place a number of abject failures. The game did not catch on in London. Nor did it have any success in South Wales. Even clubs like Blackpool Borough and Liverpool City in Lancashire, and Doncaster in Yorkshire, have at times had to struggle.

So we have nothing to celebrate, although all of us know in our heart of hearts that Rugby League is a good game, a fast open game which should be popular anywhere in Britain. The facts, though, tell us that it isn't popular.

The major trouble is, of course, the vested interests of

other sports. Association football is so deeply entrenched in most areas that it is hard to crack the wall. Rugby Union is extensively played, thanks largely to Old Boys' clubs, that there is no demand for Rugby League. People who like rugby are quite content to play or watch Rugby Union.

That is not to say that the position is hopeless, although I am convinced that we shall never live to see the day when Rugby League is a sport played all over Britain. We could, I am sure, do more to sell the game, but it is no use being stupidly optimistic. No matter how good a game is, if the public does not want it, the public will not have it; we have to admit the fact that soccer is the big winter sport of this country and that Rugby Union in all the areas outside the Rugby League 'country' is so deeply entrenched that it would be well-nigh impossible to introduce Rugby League there.

The Rugby League has tried to crash into the market by allowing the formation of clubs such as Streatham & Mitcham and Cardiff, but failure has been the reward each time. And nobody really expected anything else. It is all very well to establish a new team in a new area, but that team has got to be a good one. Those we have seen in the past have not been good ones. They have, in the main, been weak sides, sides which took beating after beating.

Now even the rabid Rugby League fans in the North will not go to watch a losing side, so how on earth did we expect a losing side in a non-Rugby League area to drag the spectators away from soccer and Rugby Union? Why must we have bad teams as our missionaries?

The ideal plan, of course, would have been to plant a strong side in London and Cardiff, but that would have meant the present clubs like Wigan, Leeds, Warrington and Huddersfield releasing some of their star players. You can imagine what the good folk of Wigan, Leeds, Warrington and Huddersfield would have said to that!

So most of our teams in the outposts have been doomed to failure simply because the teams have not been good enough to rise above the bottom of the League.

This has meant that our game has been confined within the rather narrow limits of three Northern counties, and this, in turn, has meant that our fields of publicity have been most severely restricted. I know that many Rugby League fans blame the newspapers and the B.B.C. because they do not give the game enough publicity, but the newspapers and the B.B.C. can quite easily reply that the game is not one of national popularity, and that is that. It is our job. Once we have succeeded in that object, then the publicity will follow.

One thing we need not worry about - the game itself. It is a good game, a thrilling game and an entertaining game. Put over properly there is no reason at all why we should not win many converts. But we must plan our publicity wisely and systematically.

A few years ago the B.B.C. televised the World Cup Final from Paris on a Saturday afternoon. It was a cracking match and from all over the country came reports that people had found it excellent viewing. Millions of people who had never seen a game of Rugby League had watched the televising of this World Cup Final and had been thrilled. They had received their first lesson in the appreciation of our great game and were ripe for the second lesson.

But the game had been played on a Saturday afternoon, and many Rugby League fans had stayed away from their home grounds to watch it in the comfort of their own homes. The result was that a number of clubs suffered financially, and they complained. There was a tremendous argument about the televising of this World Cup Final, and the whole of the argument centred round domestic Rugby League issues. The potential new public was forgotten.

That was a grievous mistake. One can sympathise with

the clubs that lost money, but a temporary financial loss is worth taking in view of the advantages the game could have gained from the televising of that one match. We should have been big enough to see the long-term advantages and followed up that World Cup Final immediately. We didn't, and the chance was lost.

An even greater pity is that the experience of that World Cup Final made many clubs frightened to death of television. Now television could be the death of sport as we know it in this country, but television properly used and controlled could do immense good. All sports have had the same worries since the advent of nation-wide television, but some, especially soccer, have made great progress in their co-operation with the television authorities whenever possible. Rugby League, unfortunately, has not.

Live television of Saturday league games would, it is true, be dangerous. After all, the television authorities would only wish to televise the good games - it would not be in the interests of the Rugby League to allow any of the others to go on the screen! - and this would seriously interfere with the gates at other matches. So it is doubtful whether we shall ever have television on Saturday afternoons.

But there is no reason why we should not use the light evenings at the beginning and end of the season. One match only could be played on a certain evening and that match televised. No gate would be affected, except, maybe, the gate at the actual match, and that would be covered by the television fee, and the game would be given a wide audience.

With the televising of the Challenge Cup Final and the Championship Final, that would give the great British public a fair sample of the kind of entertainment Rugby League football can provide.

Selling Ourselves

But we could not leave it there. We would have to follow up the good publicity by playing exhibition matches in various areas where reaction to the televising of matches has been good. We could send some of our best teams, or representative teams, to play special matches, and it is feasible that the people who have enjoyed the matches on television will come and have a look at the sport in the flesh.

It would, of course, be necessary to choose the areas carefully, and since the war there has been such a shifting of population that we would have no need to concentrate entirely on London and South Wales. There are now many areas of population which have sprung up since the war and which might well be ripe for development. Industry has been dispersed and new populations have grown up. Those are the places which Rugby League should attack, for in many of these towns there is no senior sport. Far better, then, to concentrate on these areas than on trying to crack the immense hold on the public which is held by such soccer teams as Arsenal, Chelsea and Tottenham Hotspur in London and by such Rugby Union teams as Cardiff, Newport and Swansea in South Wales.

By that system we should be using television sensibly. We should be giving television viewers good entertainment - for our good teams would be able to show what a fine, thrilling game we play - and we should also be doing the game itself a great deal of good by helping to spread it in fertile areas.

Far better, surely, to do something concrete instead of sitting back and moaning about television and about the lack of publicity Rugby League gets.

Just as we get the Government we deserve, so we get the publicity we deserve.

We have to go out and earn our publicity. No one is going to give it to us out of the goodness of their heart.

Rugby Renegade

6

ARE THINGS AS GOOD AS THEY WERE?

Nothing, they say, is ever as good as it was, and it is always a popular topic of conversation among football fans to discuss yesterday and today. More often than not, everyone thinks his yesterday was better than his today.

There is, of course, no yardstick by which you can judge the comparative standards of sports like football. It is not, for instance, possible to match a team from yesterday with a team from today. As a result nearly all the discussions are inconclusive, with one's opinion swayed by memory ... and one's memory is apt to play tricks. I am sure that many of the people who now talk in glowing terms of the football of the 1920s or the 1930s grumbled an awful lot at the time and compared the standard of play rather unfavourably with the standard that was common in the years before.

We have to accept the fact that in the sports where a sound judgement can be made - sports like swimming and athletics, where there are figures on which we can base our judgement - the present day wins hands down. Our swimmers are swimming much faster than they ever did in the old days. Our athletes are running faster, jumping higher and throwing longer distances than their fathers ever did. So the standard of performance at these sports has increased out of all proportion. It does not follow, however, that the standard of performance at all sports must, therefore, have increased in a like manner.

All sorts of reasons have been advanced for the vastly superior performances to which we are entertained in the swimming-baths and on the athletic tracks. Some people say the facilities are better (yet we have only two international-size swimming-baths in Britain!), that the coaching is better, that there is more competition.

What the correct reason is I do not know. But I do know that the standard of performance is much superior today than it ever was before.

Yet I am what the public calls 'an old-timer', so when I look at Rugby League I am forced to the conclusion that the standard of play today is not as good as it was before the Second World War. It could well be that I am biased because I was fortunate enough to be a member of a team that was the best in the League before the war, a team that would always rank as one of the greatest teams of all time. It may seem like boasting, but the Salford team of the 1930s played superlative football, and when one has been a member of such a combination it is always difficult to make a fair assessment of other teams.

But it is true to say that the general standard in pre-war days was very high, and that taking the league as a whole the standard of play was superior to that of today. Things were made easy for us because there was less tampering with the rules in my playing days pre-war, whereas since the end of the war the rules have been changed so often that most of the players have been confused. Fortunately, however, there has been a more static outlook by our rule-makers during the past two seasons, and this has led to a much more settled state of affairs in the game and to an improvement in play. Maybe, then, we are on the way back to the standards we knew before the war.

There are people who will tell you that the present-day player falls short of his pre-war counterpart in all aspects of the game, and I have heard it said that in no department has the standard dropped so much as in goal-kicking. The figures, however, prove otherwise. Before the war, no more than three or four players kicked a hundred goals in a season. Last season, some ten players reached that figure, and it would be silly to say that the standard of goal-kicking is low when there are players like Bernard Ganley, of Oldham, and Lewis Jones, of Leeds, in the game.

It is only fair to point out, though, that the ball used today is smaller than the ball used in pre-war days, so it is much easier to kick a goal from the half-way line than it was.

I feel that what the game lacks today is tactical execution, or, to put it in another way, the expert execution of every move. Pre-war, if a move broke down we would try it again and again until we performed the move correctly. Today the players don't. They seem to get discouraged more easily, and they are not as capable of learning from their mistakes. Often you see the same errors made time and time again in a match.

It is, however, unfair to blame the youngster too harshly for this. Youth-baiting is a popular sport today, but then it always has been. The youths of the 1930s were accused of all sorts of irresponsible nonsense, yet it was those same youths that performed so magnificently during the war. Young people of today are also accused of all sorts of irresponsible nonsense, but in all probability you will find that when the present-day youngster is put to a severe test he will come through with flying colours.

Rugby Renegade

It is not true that the young Rugby League player will not work as hard as his predecessor. If the youngster likes the game, is keen and has the talent he will work just as hard as his father worked. He will train just as hard and he is just as willing to learn. True, there are exceptions. There are lads who think they know it all after they have scored their first try. But then there always were such lads.

What we must remember is that today the youngsters have more to occupy their minds than had their fathers. Life is much fuller today than it ever was, and there are so many forms of amusement and entertainment laid on for the people. In the old days, lads had to organise their own football, and there was not the distraction of television and suchlike to take them away from the game. Nor were so many sports within the reach of the youngsters.

Furthermore, there was unemployment, not full employment, in the pre-war days, and many a man was only too glad to play football - either soccer or rugby - and pick up a few pounds. Today conditions are different. Youngsters are not tramping the streets looking for work. They are working, and mostly in well-paid jobs. There is not the same desperate need to earn that extra money from football which made all the difference in the 1930s.

A young lad drawing a good wage from some factory or other is not going to risk injury with the same careless abandon as did his father, who was probably struggling to find even a poorly paid job. The modern youngster's attitude is, 'I am in a good job and drawing good money, so why should I play football to pick up a spot of pocket money?'

You cannot blame the lads for that, and, indeed, such a state of affairs may not altogether be bad for the game. Maybe we are not getting so many young lads wanting to play rugby, but what we lack in quantity we could well be making up in quality. For only the really keen lads will now turn to Rugby League, and it is the really keen lads that we want.

The Rugby League junior movement is as strong as it ever was, and there is a flow of young players coming into the game. Many of the senior Rugby League teams have adopted the sensible policy of taking over the junior clubs as nurseries, and this can only lead to good. The young players will get the proper coaching and they will see their big chance looming on the horizon. If they are keen and talented enough they will seize that chance.

So while the present standard of Rugby League is not as high as it was - and here you must make allowances for my natural bias and my natural tendency to compare everything with that great Salford side of pre-war days - the future does look bright. The young lads are being coached and trained, there is now less chopping and changing with the rules, so we can look forward to a gradual improvement in the game.

I hope so.

Rugby Renegade

7

STOP TAMPERING

The life of the would-be reformer is always difficult. He has to convince a doubting public that his ideas are good ones, that the present way of life would be vastly improved by the introduction of changes.

There are some people who are such stick-in-the-muds that they believe all changes are wrong. There are others at the opposite end of the scale - they believe that any alteration must be for the better.

Neither of those groups is correct, and damage is done when the would-be reformer comes up against either of them. What we want is the sensible, middle-of-the-road group; the group which will examine every suggested change on its merits, which will be willing to take sensible risks, but which will never advocate change just for the sake of change.

Sad to say, Rugby League has been plagued with both extremist groups from time to time, and has suffered as a consequence. Take, for instance, the play-the-ball rule. Since the war there have been so many changes to it that we almost reached the stage when not a soul in the game - player, referee, official or spectator - knew which rule was in existence!

The play-the-ball rule has been Rugby League's problem child for years, and we have never got on top of it. Somehow or other, a sensible restart to the game must be found when a man is tackled, and the Rugby League administrators have permutated all the offshoots of the basic rule - that the man who has been tackled must be allowed to get to his feet and restart the game by playing the ball with his foot. We have stipulated that colleagues of the tackled man must be all sorts of distances from him when the ball is set in motion again. We have stipulated all sorts of distances to which the player of the tackling side must retire. And yet we have still not solved the problem.

The basic trouble with the play-the-ball rule is that it favours the man who is tackled, and it is possible, by using this rule effectively, to shut up a game. In other words, the weak side can beat the strong side merely by not releasing the ball. There is nothing to stop a team going on to the field with the orders not to let the other side have the ball. They can refuse to engage in any passing movements once they have won possession; by doing so they will slow the game, prevent any constructive movements and make the whole thing a wretched bore for all those playing and watching it. Later on I will tell how Workington Town did just that in one memorable match with Wigan.

The plan is simplicity itself. All that happens is that a man is tackled in possession - he has, remember, made no effort to pass the ball so there is no chance of the other side gaining possession by an interception. As soon as the tackle is made, the game stops. The tackled man must, by rule, be allowed to get back on his feet, and then he must restart the game by dropping it and playing it with his foot. He can - and in practice he always does! - backheel it to a colleague, who then retains possession of the ball until he is tackled and the whole dreary business starts again.

By using these tactics a team can keep the ball for minutes on end, and prevent the other side playing football.. Surely that is not what was intended?

But how do we make such tactics impossible? Some people have suggested that when a man is tackled he should give the ball to his tackler and allow him to 'play it'. That, though, is an artificial way out of the deadlock. Just as a boxer should only lose his championship in the ring, so should a rugby player only lose the ball by having it taken from him. It is completely contrary to the spirit of the game for a player to give the ball to an opponent.

Other people have suggested that Rugby League should adopt the Rugby Union system whereby the tackled man releases the ball and gets out of the way while the rival forwards try to heel it back to their own colleagues. But the Rugby Union system is little or no improvement on the Rugby League system. The loose scrum is just a conglomeration of human bodies and is dreadful to watch. After all, no one wants a scramble.

At the back of any change in the rule should be the desire to give the side which has brought off the tackle some sort of a chance. At the moment the whole of the advantage is given to the side whose player is tackled, with the result that we can get a jerky game of stop-go-stop-go.

But how different it would be if the man tackled had to get to his feet, put the ball on the ground and kick it in any direction except backwards. That would mean that he could play the ball either forwards or sideways and both teams would have an equal opportunity of gaining possession after a tackle. It would then be impossible for any player to close up the game by allowing himself to be tackled.

This reform of the play-the-ball rule would, I am convinced, speed up the game, make it more enjoyable for all concerned, and remove one of the greatest cancers Rugby League has ever experienced.

An amendment to the play-the-ball rule is just one of the two reforms that Rugby League needs. The other is the introduction of the two-divisions system. At the present time there are thirty teams in the league. It is, therefore, impossible for all the clubs to meet each other twice, and this gives an artificial appearance to the championship. Each club plays thirty-six matches, and the top four clubs play off for the title of champions. In the semi-final, the leading club is at home to the fourth club, the second club at home to the third. The winners of the semi-final then meet on a neutral ground to decide the championship.

In the 1956-7 season, Oldham defeated Hull 15-14 in the final, and these two clubs had finished first and second in the league table. But it doesn't always happen that way. In 1955-6, Hull, who finished fourth, beat Halifax, who finished second, in the final 10-9.

Although the semi-finals and final are money spinners, the present system is all wrong. The only solution is the establishing of two divisions. The idea has been suggested regularly over the last few years, but by the rules of the Rugby League it must obtain a two-thirds majority before it can become law. This it has never done because the weaker clubs are all against the introduction of two divisions.

It is only fair to understand their reasons. They feel that if they were put into a Second Division their gates would drop for two reasons: (1) that nobody likes to watch second-class anything, and (2) they would be robbed of attractive fixtures against the better teams.

But these smaller clubs are barking up the wrong tree,

and if Rugby League is to survive, the two-divisions system must be introduced. One has only to look at the Rugby League table to see the reason. In 1956-7, Doncaster won only three of their thirty-eight games. Dewsbury won five, Batley eight, Liverpool City nine. At the other end of the scale, Oldham won thirty-three. The competition is, therefore, hopelessly lopsided, with most of the clubs having not the slightest chance of winning the championship. Furthermore, the championship is artificial because all the clubs do not meet each other - my own club, Salford, for instance, did not play ten of the Yorkshire sides in the 1957-8 season.

Many of the Rugby League games are one-sided and therefore boring to watch and play, but if there were two divisions we would get much better and closer competition, and before long the standard of play would undoubtedly improve. The clubs relegated to the Second Division would find themselves in their own class, and they would have something to play for - promotion. Today they have nothing to play for at all. Instead of being thrashed unmercifully by such giants as Oldham, Barrow, Wigan and Leeds, teams like Doncaster would be meeting teams of their own strength. They would win more matches, play in much closer-fought games, and consequently the season would be much more enjoyable and exciting, both for their players and for their spectators.

No one can accuse me of advocating two divisions because my own club is at the top of the league. Salford, at the moment, are not giants of Rugby League, and if the two divisions had been formed after the 1955-6 season we would have been put into the Second Division. In 1956-7 we finished thirteenth, so we would have been a borderline case.

Two divisions, with fifteen clubs in each division, would

call for twenty-eight league games, which, with the Challenge and the County Cups, would provide a season of eight matches fewer than at present. But that would not be a bad thing because the season today stretches from the beginning of August until the middle of May. A reduction would not be all that bad! If anyone thinks a reduction of eight matches too drastic, we could always introduce a knock-out cup competition for each division.

Apart from the modification of the play-the-ball rule and the introduction of the two divisions system, Rugby League needs no changing. The game is a good one, thrilling to play and entertaining to watch. It must be kept free from the too-ardent reformers. We must stop incessant tampering with the rules and constitution. As it stands the game is one of the best spectacles in British sport, and when two good teams are playing there is nothing better to watch. Believe me: it is just as wonderful to play.

The rules are not as involved as some people imagine, and we must stop the would-be reformers introducing all sorts of little trimmings which will lead to complications. There is, for instance, no need to change the present set scrum for the line-out of Rugby Union. Actually the line-out has been tried in special exhibition games and it was decided that a change would be no improvement.

At one time, Rugby League people had the floodlight mania, but whereas floodlighting has succeeded in soccer, it has failed in Rugby League. The public just hasn't been interested in going to matches in the cold of a winter's night, and even though attractive representative fixtures - and even international matches - have been played under lights, the idea has flopped. The crowds have stayed at home.

No, Rugby League is a great game, a game the public wants to see on Saturday afternoons. And if the play-the-ball rule is amended so that the ball must be played in any direction except backwards, and if the league is split into two divisions with promotion and relegation of two, three or four clubs each season, more and more of the public will want to watch our great game.

Rugby Renegade

8

WEMBLEY IS DIFFICULT BUT . . .

Why do so many big games at Wembley turn out to be flops?
They do you know. All too often the pre-match glamour and
ballyhoo which precedes a Rugby League Challenge Cup
Final or an F.A. Cup Final is shattered by a game that is a big
disappointment to everyone. The reason is that Wembley
Stadium is a most difficult ground to play on, and that
when Cup Final day comes around the players are faced
with conditions which have become entirely foreign to
them.

The football season in England provides a set of playing
conditions which does not vary from one year to the other.
The season opens in August when the grounds are well
covered by a thick carpet of grass. Gradually that grass is
worn away and along comes the mud and the slush. Then we
get the ice and snow, with bone-hard surfaces, followed by
more mud and slush. Towards the end of the season, we go
back to firm, dry grounds which are, by now, almost entirely
devoid of grass.

Rugby Renegade

So to the Challenge Cup Final at Wembley Stadium. Now Wembley is hardly ever used. Only a few matches take place on its lush turf each season, so on Final day the playing pitch is covered with a thick carpet of green grass ... and for weeks the lads have been playing on bare, hard grounds.

That tremendous change in playing conditions is the main reason for so many Wembley flops. It is hard to run on the Wembley turf because your studs sink deep into the pile of the carpet, and no matter how hard you try you never seem to be moving fast on the ground. Furthermore, it is extremely tiring, and that, more than anything else, explains why players play better the second time they visit Wembley.

A wonderful example of this was furnished by the Manchester City soccer club. When they played Newcastle United in the F.A. Cup Final a few years ago they ran themselves to death. Newcastle, who were experienced at Wembley, allowed the Manchester players to run around the ground, knowing full well that they would soon tire. And tire they did ... and lost.

The following year Manchester City reached the F.A.Cup Final again, and it was noticeable how they changed their tactics. They conserved their energy. They did no unnecessary running. The result was that they lasted the pace much better ... and they won.

Many people refuse to believe that Wembley can be so tiring, but I can assure them that playing Wembley is like running about all day on a thick pile carpet. That, as you can guess, would be more difficult and much more tiring than running about on a wooden or concrete floor. Your feet spring off a hard, bare surface, but they sink into the thick surface of Wembley and you have to drag them out. So every movement calls for extra effort, and that extra effort takes its toll towards the end of the eighty minutes!

To complicate matters further, Wembley always produces

a swirling wind. There is no such thing as playing with or against the wind at Wembley because it seems to blow from every direction. There is no point in looking at the flags, either. They, too, swirl round to every point of the compass.

Many is the time I have taken goal kicks towards one end and found, for instance, that the wind is coming from the left. In the second half I have assumed that the wind will be coming from the right. But not on your life. It still blows from the left. The only thing to do is use the old-fashioned method of wetting your finger and sticking it in the air. And even that is not infallible!

This swirling wind probably results from the fact that the spectators in the huge bowl are so far away from the playing arena. When you stand in the middle of the pitch you get a feeling that you are surrounded by nothing more than a great expanse of air. It is uncanny and unsettling.

The Wembley authorities could help if they would allow the Cup Finalists to have a run-out on the ground the day before the big match - say one team in the morning and the other in the afternoon. Then the players would be able to get the feel of the turf, get used to this strangeness of being surrounded by air, with 100,000 spectators apparently miles away.

But no run-outs are allowed. Which is a pity.

Wembley is also upsetting to the players because every game there is a big game, and every big game produces a nervous tension which is difficult to overcome. Everyone is keyed up for the great occasion, and mistakes are easily made by footballers who are keyed up. That is why so many passes are dropped, so many passes badly made and so many tackles misjudged in the early minutes of a Cup Final at Wembley.

Recently Wembley has been accused of being a dangerous ground, and while that might well be an exaggeration, in proportion to the number of games that are played there, Wembley does produce more pulled muscles, cartilage displacements, strained muscles and Achilles tendon injuries than any other ground.

This is entirely due to the old bogey - that thick carpet of turf. The ground grips your studs like a vice and it is extremely difficult to turn. A player moving at speed tries to swerve or turn quickly, and although the body will move, the legs stay rooted to the ground and away goes a muscle or a cartilage. Remember the three soccer players who have recently received bad injuries at Wembley? There was Walley Barnes, then Jimmy Meadows and then Colin Grainger. All went down writhing in agony after they had tried to turn quickly. Their legs had stayed put and muscles had been wrenched.

In 1939, when Salford lost by 20-3 to Halifax in the Rugby League Challenge Cup Final, Osbaldestin, the Salford full-back, leapt to catch a high ball. He caught it cleanly, landed perfectly and immediately turned to start his run. But he just sat down and looked stupefied ... the attempt at a turn had wrenched his Achilles tendon.

So that is how simple it is to sustain an injury on the Wembley turf.

But let us have no nonsense about taking the Rugby League Challenge Cup Final away from Wembley. That would be a complete disaster. For Wembley is our glamour ground, and no Challenge Cup Final would be the same if it was not surrounded by all the glamour and tradition, pomp and ceremony that is part of Wembley Stadium.

Playing at Wembley is as much a burning ambition with all Rugby League players as it is with soccer players. They know it is difficult to play on the ground. They know it is a tremendous strain, both mentally and physically, but they still regard a visit to Wembley as the greatest honour in the game.

Those who would take the Rugby League Final away from Wembley point to the fact that the game is confined to the North of England, and the good that might come from the publicity of playing the Challenge Cup Final in the South is more than outweighed by the bad that is done in making the working folk of the North spend their hard-earned money on a trip to Wembley. And make no mistake about it, it costs a lot of money to get to the Stadium from the North.

Nevertheless, I believe that none of our supporters would miss the trip for worlds. Many people save up all the year round for the annual pilgrimage to Wembley, and they prefer to have the Final played on the premier sporting arena in the country rather than on one of our grounds in the North. (And let us face it, only Odsal Stadium, Bradford, of the Rugby League grounds, is big enough to house the Final.) There is still a thrill about a trip to Wembley which no one can describe, and nowhere in England can you find a better setting for a Challenge Cup Final than at the Empire Stadium.

So, despite the cost, despite the necessity of a long journey outside the Rugby League area, the fans love going to Wembley as much as the players.

No more talk, then, of taking the Final away from the great, yet difficult, Stadium.

Rugby Renegade

9

MR. RUGBY LEAGUE

Wherever or whenever people discuss Rugby League, the name of Lance Todd must crop up in the conversation. For here was the greatest character who ever graced the game of rugby, a personality comparable to such as Herbert Chapman in soccer.

Toddy, as he was known throughout the game, was a New Zealander who had played for the All Blacks. In 1928 he became manager of Salford, and it was under his inspired leadership that Salford became the team of all talents. He moulded the team into one of the greatest forces Rugby League has ever seen, and he guided the club to victory in every possible competition.

Before long he became more than a manager. He was Rugby League itself. When the B.B.C. wanted someone to broadcast about the game they called upon Toddy, and hard as the B.B.C. may have tried in recent years, they have never been able to replace him as a broadcaster on the game. And hard as the game has tried since his death, it has never been able to discover another Lance Todd.

Like all great leaders and great managers, Toddy was a strict disciplinarian. He had no favourites, and when he laid down a rule he assumed that everyone would obey it. No one ever disobeyed him twice!

He wore glasses, and a visit to his office was a positive ordeal. He would peer at you over his glasses, weigh you up carefully and then speak. And when Toddy spoke it was the voice of the law! His crackling, clear voice would rap out the orders and that was that.

He was, of course, a supreme individualist, and like all individualists he clashed fiercely with others of the same temperament. Emlyn Jenkins, for instance, was one of the finest half-backs you could wish to see on a football field, but Emlyn had his own individual style of play. It did not always coincide with Toddy's ideas, and the two of them had many a strand-up argument. They would row like demons, but each respected the other deeply. Emlyn knew that he was arguing with the finest manager you could find. Toddy knew that he was arguing with just about the finest half-back you could find.

I never had the nerve to answer back to Toddy. I often wanted to argue about the game with him - Toddy would discuss the game of rugby for hour upon hour - but each time I tried the words refused to come out of my mouth!

Many is the time I - and many tougher characters - have been near to tears after a bout of the Todd tongue. He never believed in sparing anyone's feelings, and his dressing-room pep talks were something that should have been recorded for posterity. Often I came into the dressing-room after pulling my heart out and doing my very best, but it was not good enough for Toddy. He would immediately set to and run through every mistake I had made.

For Lance Todd was a perfectionist, and he couldn't

really see why everyone else was not a perfectionist as well. Each half-time, and at the end of every game, Toddy would stride into the dressing-room and amaze us with his capacity for remembering every little incident which had taken place during the match. Even the smallest knock-on would be remembered, and he would trace a movement back to its start and lecture us on what we should have done.

So many people judge a game of football on the score. They are willing to say, 'Well, we won, didn't we?'

Toddy never believed in that philosophy. We could be fifteen points in the lead at half-time, yet Toddy would still come into the dressing-room and play hell about our mistakes. He would be able to remember each penalty kick and want to know why those of us who had taken them had neither scored nor found touch, for to Toddy a penalty kick was useless unless you scored or placed the ball into touch near the opponents' line.

But that was what made Lance Todd such a great manager. He was a driver, he got that extra something out of his men which made the difference between being champions and being runners-up, he tightened everyone so that we were all rarin' to go and do even more than our best.

He was an exceptional student of the game, and there wasn't a move he did not know from A to Z. He never allowed his concentration to relax for a second, and this was not only invaluable to him as a manager but also as a broadcaster. He knew so much about the game that he was almost ahead of the play when he was giving one of his running commentaries. The fact that he was commenting on players other than those of his own team did not worry Toddy. He made a point of knowing every player in the Rugby League and analysing both his strong and weak points. He could almost tell you what any particular player would do in any given circumstance ... and he would then tell you what that player should have done! Yes, Toddy was a perfectionist, an expert, a driver, a strict disciplinarian. But he was also a great psychologist.

When he had built Salford into the great team it was in the 1930s, when he had surrounded himself with a team that was composed of internationals or near internationals, he was content to let us train as we liked. We would be out on the field practising various moves and tricks, and Toddy would stand on the balcony outside his office and watch like an eagle. He never said anything. He knew that every man was training properly. Anyone who didn't would soon be swapping the red jersey of Salford for that of another club!

When the Second World War broke out and big-time football was suspended, Lance Todd devoted his time and energy to the Home Guard, in which he attained a high rank. And it was while returning from a Home Guard duty that he was involved in a car crash and killed.

So sport in general and Rugby League in particular lost a great man, a superb manager and an unforgettable character.

10

THE RED DEVILS

Mention the Red Devils around Salford at the present time and people will think you are talking about Matt Busby's great soccer side, Manchester United. But in the 1930s things were different. Manchester United were a struggling side, missing relegation to the Third Division by the narrowest margin and being so hard-up that one Christmas week the players received a turkey instead of wages.

The Red Devils of the 1930s were Salford, probably one of the finest rugby sides ever to appear in either code of the game. The Salford side of the 1930s was the Arsenal of Rugby League. It was all that Manchester United soccer team is today.

Lance Todd was the brains behind the side. He meant to give the city of Salford, a city which borders on Manchester and which far too often is regarded, by those who don't know, as a mere suburb of Manchester, the finest-ever Rugby League side. He did more than that. He gave Salford probably the finest rugby team that has ever appeared in regular competition.

Rugby Renegade

He had the advantage of knowing that Salford is a Rugby League city. It is the largest city in England without a first-class soccer team, and the citizens have been brought up from childhood on the game of rugby.

Toddy decided they should see the greatest rugby players of the day, and the citizens of Salford were entertained by a team composed of just that - the cream of the rugby world. It was not only a pleasure to play in the side, it was an honour. There was: Osbaldestin at full-back, a three-quarter line of Barney Hudson, Sammy Miller, myself and Bob Brown, those uncanny half-backs Emlyn Jenkins and Billy Watkins, and forwards like Bert Day, Billy Williams and Jack Feetham. It was a team of international stars who blended together as a team and formed a power machine such as the Rugby League had never seen before, has never seen since and may never see again in the future.

The Busby Babes had nothing on Toddy's Toddlers, as the team was called in the days when we were all youngsters being groomed for stardom. Gradually our side was built up over the years from 1929, and although there were one or two alterations, such as the introduction of Alan Edwards, the team remained pretty much the same.

Lance Todd could never stand mediocrity, and he made sure that no hint of it crept into the Salford side. Only first-class players would do for him, and consequently the Salford public was treated to such a feast of rugby that they became a most critical public. They followed the Todd line - only the best will do.

Nearly the whole Salford side was capped at one time or another and, as I shall tell later, I once had the honour of leading an international side on to the field followed by four of my Salford colleagues - Alan Edwards, Barney Hudson, Emlyn Jenkins and Billy Watkins.

During the 1930s Salford won the Rugby League

championship three times - in seasons 1932-3, 1936-7 and 1938-9. In 1933-4 we were runners-up. We went to Wembley on two occasions - 1938 and 1939. On the first occasion we defeated Barrow in a thrilling game 7-4, the winning try being scored in the last minute, but the following year we were not so successful. Halifax really thrashed us by 20-3.

No excuses, but Salford were a flu-ridden team that day. Half the team were not 100 per cent fit. To make matters worse one of Toddy's brain-waves came unstuck when he had the team training out in the country for a day during the week prior to the Cup Final. It was grand running about in the meadows, but not so good when we found no baths available in the barn in which we 'stripped'. A number of us caught colds which could not be shaken off by the Saturday of the game.

We won the Lancashire League in 1932-3, 1933-4, 1934-5, 1936-7 and 1938-9, the Lancashire Cup in 1934-5, 1935-6 and 1936-7. In 1938-9 we were beaten in the final by Wigan, who were, strangely enough, our opponents in all our successful finals.

Perhaps a team of all talents should have won more honours than three championships and one Challenge Cup Final in seven seasons, but like all successful clubs, Salford were everyone's target. With each club in the league wanting to beat us, we found that each successive game was just like a Challenge Cup or Championship Final. No matter which team we played, our opponents always turned out their very best form, for a victory over Salford was something to boast about.

Many are the great memories of those days, memories of thrilling battles, of exciting tries, of tremendous success - and sometimes of heartbreaking failure. But always Salford fought and played hard. Never did we let up ... Toddy would never let us! In one match against Halifax, for instance, we were fifteen points in the lead at half-time, but no one ever dared suggest we rested on our laurels. We played just as keenly in the second half, and Emlyn Jenkins even collided with the goalpost when scoring a try after half-time and had to be taken to hospital with a badly damaged shoulder. That was the Salford spirit. We never eased up.

We even beat touring sides, and I remember one game against the Australians when people said that we were being paid what would then have been a fantastic bonus to beat the visitors. Lance Todd soon put everyone's mind at rest about that. He told the newspapers: 'Win, lose or draw, it will make no difference. Our players will get just the same fees. They are going to play their normal game and make the match as spectacular as possible.'

A touring side, a team at the top of the league or a team at the bottom of the league, Salford's plan was always the same - play fast, open football and thrill the spectators with Rugby League at its best.

And it worked in that game with the Australians, for we won 16-9 and became the first Salford team ever to beat a touring side. The year - 1933.

The Rugby League thought so much of the Salford side that it decided to send us to France as the first club ambassadors to that country. That was in the 1934-5 season, and since Salford's visit Rugby League has gained greatly in popularity in France. We found even in 1934 that their spectators loved the game, especially when it was played in a spectacular fashion; in our first match against a Paris XIII in Paris the crowd simply rose to us. We led 31-15 at half-time and finished up winners by 51-36 - eighty-seven points in eighty minutes of football ... and that on a heavy ground, too.

The spectators loved it, and although the game was played the day after we had beaten Wigan in a thrilling and strenuous Lancashire Cup Final - yes, we travelled to Paris immediately after the game and played the very next day - we enjoyed it, too. I enjoyed it particularly because I scored twenty-one of the Salford points, including a goal from well inside the Salford half!

Professionalism had only just started in France at the time, and we discovered that there was a dreadful row going on between the new professional body and Rugby Federation which represented the amateurs. The Rugby Federation banned the professionals from all amateur grounds and so our match had to be played on an old race-course at La Courneuve, a few miles from the centre of Paris, while an amateur game between Stade Francais and Biarritz took place in the main stadium of Paris.

To make matters even more difficult, our game was not advertised in any of the newspapers, but the French public heard about it and seven thousand people turned up at our match, which was double the attendance at the amateur game!

At Beziers, no ground was available. The local Rugby à Treize dug up a vineyard, levelled it, and both teams played in a veritable dust-bowl, with not a blade of grass on the pitch! We won this game by forty points. One of the Frenchmen scored a consolation try by dodging among the crowd on the touch-line before grounding the ball. The touch judge was non-existent!

The French have progressed considerably at Rugby League, or Rugby à Treize, as they call it. They are spectacular players, and while they don't like hard tackling, their forwards can be quite tough enough, thank you. Generally speaking the French loved the open game rather than the forward battles, and our visits to their country during the years between 1933 and 1939 were always popular with the Salford players.

Rugby Renegade

Not only did we have some fine tussles on the field in front of appreciative spectators, but the French hospitality was ... well, just French hospitality. The power behind Rugby League in France in those days was Maurice Blein, a magnificent sportsman who worked himself into the ground for the game. That the French have taken to Rugby League so well is the greatest reward Maurice could have had.

Helping Maurice Blein was Jean Galia, one of the greatest forwards France has ever had in either Rugby League or Rugby Union. Jean Galia was a pioneer of Rugby à Treize in France, and his club side, Villeneuve, became one of the finest in the game. But Jean Galia met an untimely death while still a young man. His widow has graced many R.L. Finals at Wembley as the guest of the English Rugby League. His is a name which will never be forgotten.

It was from France that we brought a French poster proclaiming the Salford team as 'Les Diables Rouges'. That is how we got our name of 'The Red Devils'.

But back to Salford. What was the secret behind all our success? In actual fact there was no magical formula. We had the finest manager the game has ever seen, a disciplinarian, a master tactician and a perfect judge of a player. We had players who knew the game and who had a team spirit which can never have been bettered in any sport.

We worked hard on tactics, and those of you who have seen films of American rugby with their moves dictated by numbers - you know the sort of thing, 'twenty-four, thirty-six, forty-eight' - will be surprised to know that we had the same system at Salford in our great heyday. We used the numbers from one to seven, and each number meant a certain move which we had practiced, practiced and practiced until each and every one of us knew it backwards. If one plan was failing to bring the desired result we could switch to one of our other plans by the mere mention of a number.

In other words, Salford were a well-drilled, highly-skilled team composed of star individuals. That - and only that - is the secret of success in any sport.

Team spirit without competent players is as useless as star players without the team spirit and team plan.

You must have the players, you must have the plan and you must have the team spirit.

Otherwise you cannot have the success.

Rugby Renegade

11

THE FIVE-YEAR PLAN

The end of the war meant that players of my age had to consider the future carefully. We had all grown older, and we had to decide what to do with the years we had left in the game.

Returning from abroad, where I had served with the 1st Airborne Division, I picked up the threads of my Rugby League career with Salford, a team which had disbanded during the war. Now it was rising again from the ashes, and Toddy was no more. He had been killed in a motor accident.

A new name had, by this time, been added to the list of Rugby League clubs - that of Workington Town. In what one might call the outpost of the Rugby League Empire, this club was carrying the banner for the Rugby League game, and in January, 1946, I was approached by the directors of the club, under the leadership of the chairman, Mr. Meageen, and asked whether I would be willing to take over as manager.

It was big decision to make, but it dawned on me that by going to Workington I would have a chance of learning the managerial side of the game. After all, I couldn't go on playing for ever. The directors of the Salford club were most helpful. They agreed to release me, and it was decided that I should join Workington Town as the player-manager at the start of the 1946-7 season. As things turned out I joined them after leading Great Britain on that highly successful tour of Australia in the summer of 1946. In fact, as manager of the club, I arranged my own transfer as a player!

At that time things were tough in Workington. The club had to fight for itself, raise its own finance, and it didn't even have a ground to itself. It shared the Workington soccer ground, and the reserve team had to play on the greyhound track which adjoins the soccer ground. These games took place at the same time as the soccer games, and perhaps it was a miracle that sometimes there were a couple of hundred spectators watching the Workington Town reserves!

But if things were tough, there was no lack of enthusiasm, and Workington Town Rugby League Football Club had behind it the knowledge that Cumberland had been for years a hotbed of the game. That might sound surprising when you consider that there were no first-class teams in the county. But Cumberland had always produced fine players, and many is the time that in the County Championship Cumberland had beaten the strength of Yorkshire and Lancashire. And if we delve into the players produced by Cumberland we ... well, we don't need to look any further than Martin Hodgson, of Swinton, Sammy Miller, of Salford, Jim Lewthwaite, of Barrow, or Jimmy Lomas, do we? It was Lomas, a Salford player, who captained the first side ever to tour Australia.

There were a large number of junior clubs in Cumberland, and George Plummer was probably the hardest-working Rugby League councillor the game has ever known. He lived and breathed Rugby League, and it was mainly though his tremendous efforts that the Workington Town club was formed and elected into the league. To George Plummer every junior player was a potential international until proved otherwise. It amazed me to think that the lads of Cumberland had been playing Rugby League with so much keenness without the spur of a senior side in the county. But the Cumbrians love their sport, and the lack of a senior team meant nothing to them.

But when a team was elected into the senior league, the whole of Cumberland rallied round it. Everyone was determined to make the club a success and overcome the biggest handicap - the fact that Workington was so far away from any other Rugby League centre, thus putting on the club's shoulders a huge bill for travelling expenses.

Perhaps one can understand the men, who had always followed the sport keenly, supporting the club, but the most pleasing development in Workington was the way the women rallied round. They came to the matches with the men, and Workington soon became the family team. Certainly no club could have wished for more wonderful support from the ladies, God bless 'em!

As soon as I joined the club I was asked how long it would take to get Workington Town to Wembley. Well, that was a terrible question that not even the managers of such strong sides as Wigan, Leeds and Warrington would have cared to answer. I didn't care to answer it, either, so I chose my words carefully and told my Board and the public that it would take at least five years to get together a team which would, at least, be capable of reaching the Challenge Cup Final. I could promise nothing more than that.

A quick look at the team told me that there were certain weaknesses that would have to be eliminated before we could become a force in the league, but it was obvious that I had around me a keen bunch of young players who were willing to work and train. There was also a grand Board of Directors, and these directors were prepared to do anything to help. So, too, were the members of the Supporters' Association, who ran all sorts of efforts to raise the necessary finance. There were dances, raffles and goodness knows what, and the Workington Town club should be eternally grateful for the wonderful work that was done by those people in the early days, work which meant a lot of financial help to the parent club.

Secretary Hughie Bann was like a father to me in those early days, giving me a lot of good advice about local customs and prejudices. He helped me enormously when I received a scurrilous letter from someone who suggested that all Welshmen should go back where they belong - to Wales!

Keen as the young local lads were, it was obvious that Workington would need some experienced players, and I was fortunate enough to sign a couple of Australians, Tony Paskins, a centre three-quarter, and Johnny Mudge, a second-row forward. Those two players were destined to play a great part in the rise of Workington Town.

Naturally, they did not click right from the start, but once they had settled down after about half a season they became a tremendous force. With their help the team improved, and the enthusiasm for Workington Town throughout Cumberland grew by leaps and bounds. Slowly but surely the team got better and better, and the babes of the Rugby League steadily grew into strapping adults. Our league position kept improving - 19th, 11th, then 5th.

And many people kept wondering ... would the five-year plan pay off? Would Workington Town have a team capable of reaching Wembley by 1951?

12

CHAMPIONS

The moment I gave my opinion that it would take at least five years for me to gather a team capable of taking Workington Town to Wembley I forgot all about it. After all, there are more important things to do when you are the manager of a football club than wonder how your forecasts are going to turn out.

Actually, I never meant to make a forecast at all. I just wanted to impress upon the supporters that success cannot be achieved in five minutes, and I meant them to understand that although it would take five years to build a team capable of lifting one of the honours of the game, it did not necessarily follow that the team would actually win either the Challenge Cup or the League Championship.

The people of Workington, however, did not look at it that way. They were looking forward to victory in five years' time, and I was shocked to discover during the 1950-1 season that people were speculating on the success or failure of my alleged Five-Year Plan! There was no such plan, but the team was doing well and it became obvious that we would be strong challengers for a position in the top four, which meant a place in the Championship play-offs. We kept up our challenge and at the end of the season we had won a place in the top four for the first time in the history of the club.

We were called upon to play Wigan at Central Park, a formidable task for any club. And what a game it turned out to be! They still talk about it in both Workington and Wigan, but it is not really the quality of the football they discuss but the tactics I ordered during the game.

We knew that Wigan would be a tough side to beat if ever there was one, and when Bill Ivison was injured in the first half, leaving us with twelve men, our task looked pretty hopeless. But in the second half we got into the lead by a single point. I moved up to make the extra man and Happy Wilson managed to go over for a try. Johnny Lawrenson kicked the goal and we were leading 8-5.

There were fifteen minutes to go, and I realised that a one point lead was not sufficient for the twelve men of Workington against the thirteen of Wigan. So I used the laws of the Rugby League game to help us to win.

In that season, when a man was tackled he had to get to his feet and play the ball. Usually this meant a back heel to a colleague, and as no opposing player could approach within three yards, there was pretty little chance of losing the ball from a play-the-ball move.

Knowing that, I ordered that my team should retain possession of the ball at all costs. There must be no kicking, no attempts at starting a passing movement. We just had to hold on, be tackled, play the ball to a colleague, who must then retain possession of the ball until he was tackled. And so on.

So the game - if you can call it that - went on its boring

yet sensational way. Johnny Mudge, Jimmy Hayton and Jimmy Waring were all magnificent in keeping the ball. They would be tackled, play the ball to the acting half-back, who would move forward two yards and then go down in a tackle. He would then play the ball to the acting half-back, who would move forward two yards and then go down in a tackle. And it went on ad infinitum.

The Wigan supporters went mad. They booed, they jeered and they shouted. The Workington supporters replied with cheers.

The players? They didn't care two hoots whether the crowd cheered or jeered. They knew their orders and they knew they had to make no mistakes if the game was to be won. In fact some of the lads were laughing their heads off.

For those fifteen long, agonising minutes to the final whistle we kept possession of the ball, and when it was all over and we had won through to the final by the odd point, there was pandemonium. We were booed off the field, and the Wigan officials were up in arms. They never forgave us for years.

Now I agree with all those people who say that Workington Town didn't play football in that last quarter of an hour, but I ask you to agree that no team in the world would have attempted to play football. The chips were stacked against us and there was nothing else we could do. Possession of the ball meant everything, and we did nothing that was not provided for in the book of rules.

That the rules were poor ones had nothing to do with us. We exposed once and for all the stupidity of the play-the-ball rule, and we were responsible for a number of changes being made in that rule. But even with all the alterations there have been since that sensational game, the rule is still a bad one and it is still possible for any club to do as Workington Town did that day at Central Park, Wigan. What is more, given the same set of circumstances - a depleted team just a point ahead with fifteen minutes to go - I would give the same orders again and expose the flaws in the rule even further.

Perhaps the game against Wigan set the scene for our performances in the Final against Warrington at Maine Road, the home of the Manchester City soccer club. We were determined to show the world that we were capable of playing excellent football as well as shutting up the game, so our game with Warrington turned out to be one of the classics, for Warrington played magnificently, despite the handicap of having their winger, Albert Johnston, taken off after about ten minutes with a broken leg.

They overcame that handicap superbly and led at half-time, but we were far from downhearted when we came into the dressing-room at the interval. On the contrary, we were cockahoop, because just before half-time Tony Paskins had gone over for a try and this had given us tremendous inspiration.

As soon as we got into the dressing-room I told the players to sit down quietly, to relax and to forget all about the first half. The second half was all that mattered, and within five minutes of it starting we had got our noses in front. From that moment onwards we never looked back. Gibson had a terrific game at centre, and Happy Wilson has never played better, either before or since. He had Brian Bevan in his pocket.

Midway through the second half I began to feel that this was one of the finest Rugby League games I had ever played in, and then it began to dawn on me that we couldn't be beaten. I was standing there, alone on the vast field, and it suddenly hit me that we were going to be champions. Five years, I had said, it would take to build a team capable of going to Wembley, and here we were, just five years after the start, within a few minutes of being the champions of the Rugby League.

The realisation that I had led my team to success nearly made me swoon. Yes, honestly, I almost passed out.

But little did that vast crowd know that before the kick-off we were so nervous that two of our players almost came to blows in the dressing-room.

Rugby Renegade

13

CUP WINNERS

As champions we began the following season of 1951-2 with our tails right in the air, but although there was little or no change in our team it soon became obvious that we were to produce no repeat performance of our championship-winning run.

However, there was consolation in the fact that we seemed to be right on the ball as far as the Challenge Cup competition was concerned. Most of that progress was made without me because I had been injured at Salford and had spent a couple of weeks in Salford Royal Hospital with a bruised kidney. By the time I was fit to play again the team had reached the semi-final stage of the Challenge Cup.

We were drawn to meet Barrow at Central Park, Wigan, and I had to make a tough decision when it came to selecting the team. Should I rely on the formation that had brought us success in the earlier rounds or should I play myself? I thought for a long time before deciding to select myself, and when I look back I am convinced that I did the right thing. But thank goodness I kicked a goal in our 5-2 victory, otherwise I would probably have been blamed by everyone!

So here we were, just twelve months after winning the Championship, at Wembley for the Challenge Cup Final against Featherstone Rovers. But once again the Wigan hoodoo hung over us, and everyone in Barrow will tell you that they won that semi-final, not Workington.

For in the second half of the semi-final, when we were facing a strong wind, Barrow claim they scored a try between the posts. The referee disallowed their claim, and newspaper pictures did not help to settle the argument. Some showed the referee to be right, others showed him to be wrong.

But whatever the people in Barrow say, it was Workington Town who qualified for Wembley, and never have I known such enthusiasm. Almost every man, woman and child in Cumberland seemed determined to go to London to support us on the great day, and it is said that radio and television sets were mortgaged to raise the money for the trip.

Our supporters made the long journey in cars, in coaches, in trains, in aeroplanes and maybe in chariots as well. It was a mass exodus from Cumberland to Wembley.

I decided that the team should spend a couple of days at Clacton before moving to Richmond the day before the Final, and so great was the enthusiasm that not one employer quibbled about giving the men time off.

We went to Wembley to have a look at the Stadium on the Friday, and I knew full well that we were not allowed to have a training run on the pitch. To my mind it is a silly rule, but it is, nevertheless, a rule. All the same, I wanted the lads to get the feel of the turf, and knowing how different Wembley is to any other ground, I smuggled a rugby ball into the stadium. For half an hour we bounced the ball all over the pitch. We ran with it, we passed it and we kicked it.

Then we were spotted, and a panic-stricken official raced up to warn us off. But he was too late to stop us having the practice we wanted.

Everyone said we were certain to beat Featherstone, but I refused to look at it that way. Any Cup Final is an even-money bet, despite the clever ones who try to make one team the favourites, and any team that had knocked out Wigan and Leigh, as Featherstone had done, deserved to command the highest respect. They certainly commanded it from the Workington party.

I made no rules for the team on the Friday night. They knew they were on the eve of a most important match, so I could trust them to act sensibly. And so they did. Most of them went to the cinema, and they were all in bed early.

On the Saturday morning we had some massage and played snooker, and then off we went to the Stadium, arriving just less than an hour before the kick-off. To arrive sooner would have been silly, because there is nothing worse before a big match than to have the players getting more jittery every minute as they sit in the dressing-room for about ninety minutes.

I told the players to behave in the dressing-room as if they were preparing for an ordinary league game, but I knew that was easier said than done. I knew the lads would be attacked by that now-famous Wembley disease - nerves. But I could only hope for the best and trust that the players would remember my instructions which were to go all out on attack from the kick-off and try to break the tension with an early score.

I needn't have worried. My team didn't forget a word, and right from the kick-off we swept on to the attack. One of the Featherstone players ran offside and we were awarded a penalty kick. So it all depended on me. Could I kick the goal and put us into an early lead?

Rugby Renegade

I succeeded, and I am convinced that going into a 2-0 lead so early was responsible for our final victory.

Most teams are frightened of throwing the ball about at Wembley because they are afraid that the nervous tension will lead to mistakes and the present of a score to the opposing side. But once we had gone into the lead we had no such fears, so we gave the ball plenty of air, a thing not usually seen in a Wembley Final until at least thirty minutes have gone. Featherstone also went all out to play the open game, which meant that the spectators received good value for money.

Probably no Wembley Final has ever produced such sensational scores. In the first half, for instance, Johnny Lawrenson dribbled almost the entire length of the field, then was tackled on the line as he picked up the ball. He immediately got to his feet, played the ball and went over for a vital try. Then he fell exhausted.

In the second half, the same player made an interception inside his own twenty-five yard line and raced right to the other end of the field to score what must surely rank as the greatest try seen at Wembley.

And to prove my point about Rugby League forwards having to be able to run with the ball, unlike their Rugby Union counterparts, John Mudge, our fourteen-stone second-row forward, took a pass from Bill Ivison and raced sixty yards for a try. That is the stuff of which top-class Rugby League is made, and eventually we beat Featherstone Rovers by 18-10.

It was a hard struggle, but it was worth it to hear the cheers of our supporters after the game. And what a return home we had on the Monday. We travelled North by train and then went across country by coach from Scotch Corner. And every village in Cumberland turned out to cheer us home. When we reached Workington you could hardly get near the Town Hall, where the Mayor gave us a Civic Reception.

But on the way to Workington we paid one call every player was proud to make. We moved away from the streamers and the banners which lined our route and stopped at the house of a boy who had been crippled from birth. He could only see people through a mirror at the side of the bed in which he had to spend his whole life. But, despite his predicament, he was an ardent Workington supporter, and whenever we passed his house on the way to a game he would wave to us.

The Supporters' Association had bought him a television set prior to the Final so that he could see his favourite team in action, and we were only too glad to stop off and let him touch the Cup.

So it was the Championship one year and the Challenge Cup the next. No wonder enthusiasm in Workington had reached fever pitch. No wonder people talked about our doing the double the following season.

But, as so often happens in the game of football, fate dealt us a cruel blow in one of the opening games of the season. We were playing Wigan, and our stand-off half-back, Jack Thomas, was tackled and hurt his neck. He was taken off the field, and while the trainer was attending to him, Albert Pepperell, the scrum half-back, severed his Achilles tendon.

Both trainers ran onto the field to have a look at Pepperell, who had to be taken off, and while the trainers were on the field, Jack Thomas came back.

As soon as play restarted, Jack got the ball and threw a pass out to me. I was horrified to see that when he made the pass he never moved his neck at all. It dawned on me that something was wrong, so I kicked the ball out of play and ordered him off the field.

I was glad I did, for it transpired that he had broken his

neck, and if he had been tackled during that short period he held the ball, he could well have died. He spent six months in hospital, lying in bed with screws attaching his head to the bed. He was absolutely immobile, but, happily enough, he is now recovered and is perfectly well. He was, of course, never able to play rugby again.

Pepperell did not play again until nearly a couple of seasons after his injury, and then he broke his leg, which finished a very fine career.

The loss of these two grand players was a crippling blow from which we never recovered.

The following season, 1953-4, nearly saw me achieve a great ambition - that of equalling the record of Jimmy Hoey, of Widnes: playing and scoring in every game. I almost did it, for I played in every game and scored in all but one. That was against Oldham at Workington, where we won 3-0.

We took the lead through a try, which I had to convert to keep up my chance for the record. The ground was an absolute quagmire and I knew the kick would be a difficult one. So I took my time and took careful aim - but the ball just skimmed the outside of the post.

So a few inches robbed me of a great record, and a game against Halifax robbed the team of another appearance in the Championship Final. For that game was in the semi-final and Halifax beat us.

Halifax, then, got to the Championship Final, where they met Warrington. Curiously enough, they met Warrington in the Challenge Cup Final, too. But both times Warrington won.

A cruel game is football!

14

BACK HOME - TO SALFORD

The time comes when all footballers must say 'Good-bye' to the game they love, and it began to dawn on me during the 1953-4 season that such a time in my career was rapidly approaching. I didn't want to overstay my welcome, so reluctantly, although I am sure wisely, I decided that I would make a gradual exit from the game during the season which was due to start in the August of 1954.

This meant that Workington Town would need a new full-back, and I had already spotted the man who looked likely to take my place. He was Bill Wookey, an eighteen-year-old who was playing for the Furness Rugby Union Club.

I had first spotted him when he was fifteen, and even at that tender age he was playing in senior Rugby Union. Since that time his uncle had kept me informed about his progress, and he appeared to be such a wonderful prospect I determined that he must become a Workington Town player. My plan was to groom him personally throughout the

1954-5 season so that he would be able to take over completely from me in the full-back position.

Towards the end of the 1953-4 season, then, I decided to act. Workington Town were playing Liverpool City, but I motored to Barrow, signed Wookey and then dashed back to lead my team onto the field against Liverpool. I felt happy, for I knew I had signed a really promising player, a player who would, with the right grooming, be a decided asset to my club.

During the summer I went for a holiday to the South of France with my family, and when I returned I had the shock of my life.

I discovered that Workington Town had signed another full-back - Stan Thompson, from Dewsbury. Never before had a player been signed without my approval. Now one had been signed without my being consulted at all, and the player was obviously intended to take over from me at full-back, the job I had planned for Bill Wookey. I had nothing whatsoever against Stan Thompson, but I was upset that the directors had not consulted me about the signing.

Nevertheless, I decided to stay on as player-manager although I let the directors know exactly how I felt.

But a manager's days are numbered when the directors sign players while he has an entirely different plan under consideration. It was therefore no surprise to me when the directors began to criticise my choice of team. This was obviously more than the red light. It was the signal that the time had come for Gus Risman and Workington Town to part company. No manager can stay in his job under conditions like that.

So I offered my resignation - and it was accepted.

After I left Workington the directors played Wookey at centre three-quarter and he has done well. No representative honours have come his way yet, but he is one of the most promising centres in the Rugby League. But Wookey would have been twice the player if he had been played at full-back for three or four seasons as I intended. He could then have moved into the three-quarter line and become probably the leading centre in the game. It is a pity the directors did not see it that way.

Having accepted my resignation as the manager of the club, the Workington Town directors kindly cancelled my registration as a player so that I was free to go wherever I wished. I still lived in Cumberland - at Cockermouth, and I had a sports outfitters business in Workington - but when the chance came along to join Batley, the Yorkshire club, I gladly accepted.

I played for Batley until the Christmas of 1954, and all the time I kept receiving letters from people in Salford asking me when I was going to return to my old club. Many of the letters pleaded with me to return, and some people even telephoned my home in Cumberland. It was good to know I was remembered in Salford, but my playing days were, I felt, over.

It was obvious, though, that I couldn't keep out of the game I have always loved, for the old yearning came back to me immediately I stopped playing for Batley. The work at my business did not help me to get the old feeling out of my bones, so I took a job with a firm of soft drink manufacturers and travelled the Lancashire area.

Then Jimmy Douglas resigned as the manager of Salford, and the trickle of requests for me to go back to the Willows became a flood. Now the fans wanted me as the manager. There were letters, there were telegrams, there were telephone calls and there were personal callers. None of the requests was official. All of them came from the supporters of the Salford club. It made me feel proud to know that the folks wanted me back, that people thought I could help to restore the old glories of The Red Devils.

Rugby Renegade

I must admit that the job attracted me. After all, my heart was in the game, and I had long since realised that in my short time away from Rugby League I had suffered - as so many other people who leave the sport they love have suffered. Once football gets into your bones you cannot lose the old feeling - and football was in my bones.

At long last the post of Salford's manager was advertised. I sent in my written application, was put on the short list - and was eventually offered the job, which I took on in February, 1955, just before the first round of the Challenge Cup.

It didn't take me long to size up what was wrong with Salford. There were a number of problems, the chief of which was that the team was not knitting together. Perhaps the team spirit was not all it should have been, but team spirit often sags when a team is going through a bad spell, as Salford undoubtedly were in that period. There was a definite lack of understanding among the players, and I got the feeling that there was no set plan of tactics. However, I brought in one or two new training rules in an effort to make training and practice more interesting, and the team began to improve slightly, a fact which gave me great hope for the future.

One great deficiency at Salford was money. The club had been attracting poor gates, and while it is easy for the members of the general public to grumble, they must realise that no football club can carry on without money.

The man in the street is only too ready to ask why the club does not buy so-and-so, or sign this or the other big Rugby Union star. But all that costs money - the kind of money Salford just did not have. However, I was assured by the Board of Directors that if I found the players they would find the money. But, of course, finding the players is not quite the simple job some people outside the game think it is!

Despite the generous promise of the directors, it was

plainly obvious that money was the No. 1 need at Salford. It was the No. 1 need of many football clubs, and some of them were solving their problems by running a private lottery or football pool. The Salford Supporters' Association planned to do the same, so I decided that my first job was to give the Association all the help that was necessary.

For two or three months during the summer of 1955 we worked organising the lottery and we had our reward during the following season when our efforts met with unqualified success. Even people who could not really have cared less about the future of Rugby League football joined the Association so that they could participate in our lottery. The financial profit that has come the way of the Supporters' Association has amply repaid all the great efforts that went into organising the pool.

A great deal of that money has been handed by the Supporters' Association to the parent club, and used to brighten up the ground, which had fallen into disrepair in many places. It has also been used to sign one or two players and help put the club on a much sounder financial basis.

So let nobody be under any illusions as to what the Salford Rugby League Club owes to its Supporters' Association and its hard-working committee. These people have shown the right sort of keenness, and my earnest wish is that very shortly Salford will once again boast the sort of team such loyal supporters deserve.

The present side is young and often suffers from inexperience. But there is no easy road to success in sport, and these youngsters have to have their chance. They have to gain experience and learn the hard way. They are all tremendously keen and willing to learn, so it is now up to the supporters to be patient, to allow these young players time to develop. And during that development period the lads do need some encouragement.

Rugby Renegade

May everybody who watches Salford remember that. Rome wasn't built in a day, and neither was any successful Rugby League team. And no successful Rugby League team was ever built without encouragement from its supporters.

15

GREAT PERSONALITIES

Rugby is a team game, but that does not stop great personalities emerging from time to time. On the contrary, rugby, like all other team games, needs its personalities, men who are capable of drawing a crowd by themselves, men who are often responsible for the attendance being a thousand or two higher than normal.

Men, in other words, like the incomparable Jim Sullivan. If boxing can make out a case for calling Jim Driscoll 'Peerless Jim Driscoll', then Rugby League can make out an equally convincing case for calling Jim Sullivan 'Peerless Jim Sullivan'. For Jim Sullivan will always remain one of the greatest of all rugby players - amateur or professional, Union or League.

A Welshman, Sullivan came North to play for Wigan, and no player has ever won so many international honours. Which is not surprising, for few men can ever have loved their sport more than Jim. He simply lived for it, and it was, perhaps, this passionate love for the game which made him such a remarkable player.

Rugby Renegade

So many full-backs are either good in defence or good in attack. Hardly any are good in both departments. Yet Jim Sullivan was not only a good defender and a good attacker, but he was simply brilliant at both. He weighed fourteen-and-a-half stone, and yet he could move forward with his three-quarters and take part in all their passing movements. He was at his most dangerous when he came forward at tremendous speed on the blind side to take a pass from the half-back and dart through before anyone had realised the danger. He was incredible in those attacks, and once he had started to move it was well-nigh impossible to stop him.

But that was Sullivan, a master tactician, a great student of the game, and perhaps the most brilliant captain the game has ever known. With Sullivan in command you were playing under a general who was quite willing to do as much work as the private. He had that happy knack of keeping morale high, no matter how tough the situation, and many a Rugby League player has said that with Sullivan against you you could never be sure of victory, no matter how comfortable your lead might look.

Jim Sullivan's greatest glory was won with his kicking. It didn't matter whether it was a punt, a drop-kick or a place kick, Sullivan was always a model of accuracy. He had timing, direction and strength, and what is more he had the cunning of a fox.

In pre-war days, when there were many great kickers in the Rugby League game, rival full-backs often fought long-kicking duels. Each would try to manoeuvre the other into an error, so making it easy to find touch.

These kicking duels were like games of chess. They were fascinating to watch as two men kicked and ran and caught with incredible accuracy. Even the players used to hold their breaths wondering which full-back would make the first error.

Nobody used to worry so much when Sullivan was one of the full-backs, for he nearly always won. He was like a fox in these duels, lulling his opponent into a false sense of security and then striking at the weak spot - which he had conveniently spotted. There would be the opponent, caught on the wrong foot, going the wrong way, and Sullivan's deadly kick would be rolling into touch, gaining his side something like fifty yards. Or maybe Sullivan would intentionally reduce the length of his kicks so that his rival would have to advance to take them. It was almost like the story of the spider and the fly. The opposing full-back would move forward a few yards at a time, taking the ball cleanly each time. Maybe he would feel his confidence growing, for wasn't he kicking a longer ball than Sullivan?

And then it would come, as swiftly and as fatally as the strike of a snake. Peerless Jim would suddenly release one of his devastatingly accurate long kicks. The ball would sail over his opponent's head. His opponent would start to run backwards - then turn round and chase. But it was too late. Sullivan had tantalised him, kidded him, lured him right into the trap. And the ball would be in touch.

That was Sullivan, and if you gave Jim the chance of a shot at goal within fifty yards of the goalposts, then you could start handing over the two points. For Sullivan was an expert goalkicker. I shudder to think how many goals he kicked during his long and illustrious career, but it must be an incredible number.

But - and I know this will give rise to fierce arguments throughout the Rugby League world - I do not regard Jim Sullivan as the greatest of the distance place kickers. That title must surely go to Martin Hodgson, the big, burly forward, who gave such splendid service to Swinton and to his native Cumberland. I have heard it said that someone has kicked a goal from seventy-five yards, but I have never seen that done, and I cannot believe that anyone was so consistent as Hodgson from long distances.

Far too often we of Salford suffered from the mighty kicking of this Swinton giant, who regularly landed goals from the half-way line, and many is the Salford-Swinton 'Derby' that has turned on this fantastic goal-kicking of one of the game's most dangerous and brilliant forwards.

No chapter on the personalities of Rugby League would be complete without a mention of Bob Brown, the Salford winger. Some people remember him mainly as a character, but let no one be under any misapprehension. The Wigan-born wingman was a fine player, and one has only got to check up on the string of tries that he scored to realise that he was one of the best in the game.

The crowd loved Bob as a player, and they loved him as a character. For Bob meant to get on in the world, and it was entirely through his own efforts that he improved himself in his speech and also became known as one of the best-dressed men - if not the THE best-dressed man - in the Rugby League. He would turn up at the ground, sartorially elegant in a polo jumper, plus fours, but no stockings, and wearing slip-on sandals! His wife was just as much a pleasing character as he was. She would arrive at the ground with Bob and she nearly always carried with her a marmoset. Believe me, that marmoset became a Salford fan, too!

Bob Brown and his wife were, then, a great double act, but if you are talking of double acts there have been none to equal that of Emlyn Jenkins and Billy Watkins, the half-backs to end all half-back combinations. Jenkins and Watkins were to Rugby League what Elsie and Doris Waters, Ethel Revnell and Gracie West were to the variety stage. In Rugby League history they will be forever as famous as Olivier and Vivien Leigh or Astaire and Rogers will be in film history.

Never have I known a pair of footballers with such a complete understanding, and it was around this pair that most of our moves revolved in the Salford heyday. They practiced together until they knew each other inside out. The mere lifting of an eyebrow, the slightest movement of a finger all meant something in the Jenkins-Watkins code. So their perfect partnership, their uncanny understanding and their baffling tactics were no accident. They were just the result of sheer hard work and practice by two natural footballers.

But even players of the calibre of Emlyn Jenkins and Billy Watkins would have been completely harmless if they never received the ball, and half-backs in rugby depend a great deal on their hooker to provide them with a service. Once the hooker has got the ball out of the scrum, the half-backs can then go to town and wreak havoc to their heart's content. But if the hooker does not heel, well....

Jenkins and Watkins, then, would be the first to give praise to the man who did the Salford hooking in those days - Bert Day. Bert was the quickest striker of a ball I have come across, and it was nothing extraordinary for him to get possession of the ball from seventy-five per cent of the scrums. You can imagine how much that meant to Salford when we had half-backs like Jenkins and Watkins, and three-quarters like Bob Brown, Alan Edwards and Barney Hudson!

Barney Hudson! Now there was a wingman for you, and contrary to the general rule, the older Barney got the better player he became. As the years went on, Barney developed more speed and more precision of movement - the two main requirements for a wingman - until at the outbreak of war he was at his best. In the early days of his career he could see just one thing- the line. As soon as he received the ball he would go straight for the line, and I do mean straight. The fact that a couple of opponents were positioned between him and the line meant absolutely nothing to Barney - he would go straight through them, brushing them aside as if they didn't exist.

With age came experience and wisdom, and Hudson developed not only a sidestep but also a most devastating hand-off.

Many people always regarded him as too big for a wingman, but these people did not know their Barney Hudson. His strength was concentrated in his shoulders and his thighs, and when he was in full flight his force of impact was akin to that of a hydrogen bomb.

I remember him once in a match against Wigan. He had burst through and only the great Jim Sullivan stood between him and the line. Now Jim tipped the scales at more than fourteen stone, and he wasn't used to being pushed around by anyone. But Barney Hudson went straight at him, moved a little to one side and then hit Sullivan with a shoulder charge which sent a shudder all round the ground. Peerless Jim collapsed like a pile of bricks after someone has taken the bottom one, and Barney without even checking his stride, raced over for a try between the posts.

That was the power of Barney Hudson when he was going full tilt for the line.

Who else springs to mind? There is Jim Brough, who was probably the finest of all attacking full-backs. He was such a good attacker that he was just as good a player at centre three-quarter as he was at full-back. Many people, indeed, think he was better in the centre.

Two faults prevented his becoming as great a full-back as Sullivan, although in one international match at Hull in which he was full-back for England against Wales, who had Jim Sullivan wearing the No. 1 shirt, Brough had Sullivan running all over the field. I don't think Sullivan had ever taken such a beating, and I doubt whether he ever took one so severe afterwards. Brough even beat him at his own game - tempting him to follow-up his kicks and then over-kicking him.

But back to those faults. Brough was weak on one foot - the right foot. He could cope with anyone with his left foot, but he had neither power nor direction with his right.

Then he was such a good attacker that sometimes his defensive game suffered. Mind you, he often made up for that by following the old advice that attack is the best form of defence. His speed was phenomenal, and he loved nothing better than to race right up the field and make the extra man in attack.

Yes, Jim Brough was a great player, but, of course, a great player of yesterday, and no one wants to read only about the pre-war players. No one can blame the youngsters of today for wanting to know about the great players of the present. And no matter how hard you argue about the respective merits of yesterday and today, there is one modern player who will, I am convinced, carve for himself a niche in Rugby League history as everlasting as those carved by Sullivan and the others. That player is Billy Boston.

You may have heard of these places before: he was born in Tiger Bay, Cardiff, and he went to South Church Street School. Yes, he was born in the same place and educated in the same school as I was. But the link between Billy Boston and me goes even deeper. At one time his mother used to work for my father.

So it isn't surprising that I was the first to know about the promising talent of the coloured wonder boy from Tiger Bay - Billy Boston. I first heard about him on a trip to Cardiff. I watched him play, liked what I saw and went so far as to have a word with his parents.

Once or twice I watched him play as a schoolboy and

decided then that this was the boy I wanted to sign. Even at fifteen he had all the makings of a great player.

I dearly wanted to sign him before he was called up for his National Service, but his father thought it best for him to join the Army first, so when Billy went into the forces I continued my chase, being still determined that he should become a Workington Town player. (In passing, I wonder what the Welsh Rugby Union authorities were thinking about to allow such a great player to walk clean out of their game!)

Eventually his father agreed that he should come to Workington to meet the lads and have a look at the town. I was cockahoop. Boston, I thought, was mine.

Billy came with me to Workington and I showed him round. It was the close season, and the players of Workington Town had a cricket team. Billy even played for it during his stay with us.

At the end of his visit, I drove him one Sunday from Workington in Cumberland right down to Cardiff in South Wales. I talked and talked and talked to his father until the early hours of the Monday morning. Then I drove back to Workington without a rest, which meant that I had twenty-four hours' solid driving and negotiating.

As things turned out, Boston went to Wigan, not to Workington, and I have never made any secret of my disappointment, for he has developed into one of Rugby League's greatest personalities and into one of the finest wingers one could wish to see on any rugby field. He has speed and handling ability right out of the ordinary, and I have yet to see any player with the same ability as Boston for bursting out of a half-tackle. Many is the time opponents think they have got him nailed, but somehow or other he can throw tacklers off and not lose a split second. He is incredible and will most assuredly develop into one of the greatest players of all time providing he does not put on too much weight. This tendency to put on weight is his only trouble. Apart from that, Billy Boston has got the lot.

I am convinced that in years to come we shall talk about him at the same time as we mention wingers like Barney Hudson, Alf Ellaby, Brian Bevan and Alan Edwards.

Bevan is an Australian whose performances with Warrington have ensured for him a place in Rugby League history. He is the most enigmatic player I have ever seen, and no one I have met ever knows what he is going to do next. Like Boston, he takes a tremendous amount of tackling, for the faster he goes - and when Bevan goes he really goes! - the stronger he becomes.

His favourite trick is to use his tremendous speed for a crossfield run which leaves the defence standing still. Goodness only knows how many tries he has scored by racing across field.

Yes, Brian Bevan will always rank as one of the best of this or any other time, yet to look at him you would never think he was a star Rugby League player. He wears knee-pads and carries more strapping, padding and cotton wool than any other Rugby League player of my experience. But for all that he is a magnificent winger.

So, too, was Alan Edwards, and he was another player who didn't, perhaps, really look the part. I remember the day well when he joined Salford from Aberavon. He had long, thin legs and as we watched him walk on to the field for his first practice we all shook our heads. This man, we thought, will not last five minutes in Rugby League football.

How wrong we were! He turned out to be an incredible winger, and he was the quickest man off the mark I have ever played with or against. He was at top speed in about three strides, and his change of pace was uncanny. So, too, was his change of direction, for Edwards could sidestep, especially off his left foot, without the slightest loss of pace.

Rugby Renegade

Never shall I forget the Rugby League Championship Final of 1939. Albert Gear kicked the ball through, and in the twinkling of an eye Alan Edwards was at top speed. He caught the ball without checking his speed and simply flew down the touchline. No one had the faintest hope of stopping him, but the full-back, almost in desperation, came across, hoping, no doubt, to bundle him into touch. Edwards treated him almost with contempt. As the back closed in, Edwards sidestepped in his own inimitable style and without checking his breakneck pace went over for a magnificent try.

That was Edwards at his very best, but then he was hardly at anything else. He was a wonderful team man and had an almost fanatical keenness for the game. Once during the war I was playing for the Army against the R.A.F. , and he was in the R.A.F. side. I took an interception, and Alan came racing across from the opposite wing shouting at the top of his voice, 'Risman, you so-and-so, you're offside.'

Another fine player was Stan Brogden, who gave such splendid service to Leeds, Bradford Northern and Huddersfield. Like Edwards, he was an exceptionally fast runner with tremendous powers of acceleration. Once he got away no one stood the slightest chance of catching him. He was such a fine sprinter that he trained for the Powderhall Sprint, but his speed was well known and he never received a reasonable handicap that would give him a chance of winning.

Like any other game, Rugby League needs its match-winners, and we have one of the best of all time in the present Salford side - Wally McArthur. He has that incredible ability to turn the half chance into a try, and perhaps the best compliment I can pay him is to say he is good enough to be ranked with any of the Salford side of the 1930s.

One could go on for hours talking about the great

personalities of this great game, but there must be an end to everything. However, with the exception of Martin Hodgson, I seem to have concentrated entirely on full-backs, three-quarters and half-backs. So what of the forwards?

Well, Rugby League has produced many wonderful forwards, and I don't think there has ever been a better pack than the one we had on the 1936 tour to Australia. Its total weight was between ninety and a hundred stones!

There was Nat Silcock (of Widnes), Tom Armitt (of Swinton), Cod Miller (of Warrington), Jack Arkwright (of Warrington), Harry Beverley (of Halifax) and Martin Hodgson (of Swinton). What a mighty pack of forwards!

Arkwright was 6 ft. 3 in. tall and weighed fifteen stones. He was a huge, gangling chap, and, believe it or not, he could pick up a rolling rugby ball in one hand. I have never seen anyone else anywhere in the world do that.

But those are the sort of fellows who have helped to make Rugby League the wonderful game it is.

Rugby Renegade

The reverse pass will often send defenders the wrong way

When Martin Hodgson tackled you . . . you stayed tackled!

N.B. All photo captions are as per original book

Don't worry, it's just a camera angle. I *did* kick this goal
although it looks like a hit post

[The author] escaping a flying tackle

Can you spot me as an eleven-year-old? If not, look at the boy
holding the cup fourth from the right in the back row

Rugby League and Rugby Union players once joined forces . . . when they were
in the Forces! This is the Welsh team which played England at Gloucester on
March 28, 1942, and most of the players are Rugby League men. But Union
followers will recognise many Union stars, including Haydn Tanner, right of the
two seated players at the front.

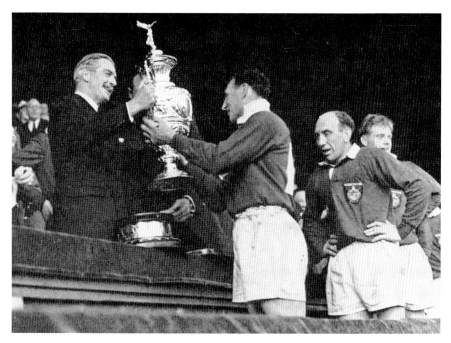

The moment I had planned . . . receiving the Rugby League Challenge Cup from Sir Anthony Eden after Workington Town's victory at Wembley in 1952

A great moment! Leading the Great Britain team on to the field at Sydney in 1936, followed by four club-mates from Salford - Alan Edwards, Barney Hudson, Emlyn Jenkins and Billy Watkins

The correct method of making a pass

Left: Signing for young autograph hunters in Australia

Above: It's difficult to pick up when you're harassed

A forward battle in Rugby League is a tough battle

A measured run-up . . . with
the eye on the ball

Perfect balance . . . with the eye
on the ball

The toe under the ball for the actual
kick . . . with the eye on the ball

The follow through - and the
ball flies straight and true

In the uniform of a Great Britain player

16

AUSTRALIA: PART ONE

Every four years, Great Britain sends its Rugby League team to Australia to play a series of Test matches and games against the club and State sides. Selection for one of these touring parties is regarded as the highest honour one can win in the game, and like everyone else, during the 1931-2 season I was hoping that I might be able to get into the party which was to make the trip in the summer of 1932.

I had already been blooded in representative football. On March 18, 1931, I won my first honour when I was chosen to play for Wales against England at Huddersfield, and three days later I was in the Glamorgan & Monmouth XIII which travelled to Whitehaven and beat Cumberland in a county game.

The day of that match was March 21, 1931, and on the morning of that day our team was called together and Jim Sullivan, who was full-back and captain (I was playing centre three-quarter), made a little speech and presented me with a fountain-pen as a gift from the players on the occasion of my twenty-first birthday. I was overcome with emotion and thanked the players profusely, but I couldn't help pointing out that March 21, 1931, was my twentieth birthday, not my twenty-first. Not a soul would believe me - they probably thought that I was a youngster getting all coy about advancing years! - and I had to keep the pen. But honestly, I was born on March 21st, 1911, so the lads gave me a twenty-first present on my twentieth birthday.

Glamorgan & Monmouth played only one more game in the county championship - in the April of that year when we were beaten by Yorkshire at Halifax - and then we moved into the all-important season of 1931-2, the season when we could make or break our chances of going to Australia.

I was in the Welsh side which lost to England at Salford in the January of 1932, and I felt that I had only a faint chance of going on the tour. After all, Jim Sullivan was a certainty for the No. 1 full-back spot, so my only hope was to be reserve full-back or fight my way into the three-quarter line.

In the final trial match I was full-back on one side with Jim Brough playing for the opposition. But Brough pulled a thigh muscle in the first half and retired at half-time. In the second half I played a blinder and won my place on the tour as deputy full-back to Jim Sullivan. I learned later that I got into the party on a casting vote, just nosing out Jim Brough.

It was an unforgettable experience to be with such a party, even as a reserve, and I don't think I realised I was on the tour until it was half over. That is how it hit a young, inexperienced player like myself.

Throughout the tour I was considered to be the utility player. Although actually chosen as the reserve full-back, I played in the less important games at full-back, centre three-quarter, scrum-half and stand-off half. In one match at Orange I played on the wing and scored three tries. That was actually my first-ever game for Great Britain, although it was not, of course, a Test match. We won by 50-9, and my most vivid memory is of the motor trip to Orange. It was a trip of a hundred and sixty-eight miles, rather tiring, but nevertheless unforgettable as we passed through the magnificent scenery of the Blue Mountains. And just to set the seal on a glorious trip, we were paraded to the ground by a band.

One really tough game on this trip was that against Metropolis on the Sydney Cricket Ground. There had been heavy rain, and the pitch was churned up into a nice muddy mess. I didn't play in the match, but remember that we won 29-5.

The match report in the fiery Sydney newspaper, *Truth*, was my first experience of this renowned journal. To call it 'fiery' is perhaps, an understatement. Just look at this, the introduction to *Truth*'s account of the game:

> Goom lads, but the beef on the hoof of Old England can play this 'ere game 'o Rugby League football!
>
> A shame, we reckon the way they treated the wee brigade of Metropolis yesterday... They mauled and manhandled them, dipped their eyes and their nether ends in the mud, slithered and slipped everywhere like eels among reeds, and handed out a trouncing to the tune of 29-5.

Everyone's ambition on a tour is to play in a Test match, but I had little or no hope of making the Test side, and sure enough I wasn't selected when we faced Australia at the Sydney Cricket Ground for the first encounter on June 6, 1932. Seventy thousand, two hundred and four people saw the game, and what a tremendous tussle it was! Right from the word 'go' Australia attacked, but Alf Ellaby made a glorious interception and raced fifty yards for a try. Then Australia got a couple of penalty goals to lead 4-3, but Ellaby made a try for Arthur Atkinson, which Jim Sullivan converted, so we were ahead again 8-4. Once again Australia hit back with a penalty goal and reduced the lead to 8-6, and that's how it stayed. The First Test was ours.

Then came a stormy set-to at Brisbane, a set-to which set the scene for the never-to-be-forgotten Second Test. We played and beat Queensland 15-10, but one newspaper called it 'an affray' and had as headlines:

'FORWARDS FOUGHT IT OUT WITH FISTS'
'LEAGUE GIANTS IN WILD MELEE'

I was full-back that day, and all I can say is that I am glad I wasn't in the pack! At one time we had only eleven players on the field.

The next game at Brisbane - the Second Test - was even worse. I was one of the reserves, and before the game someone well known in Australian Rugby circles - now a great friend of mine and one of the most respected Rugby League journalists and broadcasters in England - came into our dressing-room and started to lay down the law as to how the play-the-ball rule should be interpreted by Great Britain. He illustrated his points by using pennies on the floor, and every member of the British party was so flabbergasted at what was, after all, tremendous cheek, that nobody said a word. His lecture over, he turned round and left.

But he had succeeded in his object of leaving us in two minds, and even he would blush if he heard the things that were said about him in the British dressing-room that day!

Australia won that Second Test 15-6, but it wasn't a game of football. It was just a roughhouse. Fists kept flying so regularly that it was difficult to see how the game could finish. At times there were two or three players being attended to, and one injured player, who was taken over the touchline for attention, pleaded with the trainer not to send him back on the field.

'I'm not going back to what is going on out there,' he said.

One of the Australian journalists who had been in England said that some of the incidents in that Second Test were 'as disgusting as those which occurred in the Scotland v Wales Rugby Union international at Murrayfield last January'!

Nevertheless, some of the football in between the fist fights was excellent, especially that of Ernie Norman, the Australian half-back, who played magnificently, although concussion prevented his remembering anything of the second half.

So we went into the Final Test all square at one-all, and I got the thrill of my life when it was announced that I was to play at half-back. And I wouldn't have missed that game, played on the Sydney Cricket Ground in front of more than 50,000 spectators, for anything in the world.

Everything depended on the game. We held the Ashes, but before we knew where we were, Australia were nine points in the lead. We managed to pull that back to 9-3 by half-time, but things looked black for us.

In the second half, Stan Brogden, the left centre, and I swapped places, but that didn't seem to help for the Aussies got another penalty goal and we were 11-3 down. Defeat now seemed inevitable.

But then we got on top. Stan Brogden got over for a try and the Australians began to take the father and mother of a beating. They also adopted some strange tactics - only three

133

men in the scrum - and we suddenly got the smell of victory. I got the ball from a scrum, flung it out to Stan Smith and he was over. Sullivan kicked the goal and it was level at eleven points each. Then Sullivan kicked a penalty to put us in the lead for the first time, but this was soon neutralised by an Australian penalty.

Five minutes to go and it was 13-13. A draw was enough to give us the Ashes as we were the holders, but in this electric sort of game you just had to go all out for a win.

With the minutes ticking away, I saw another chance. Out went the ball to Stan Smith, and over went Stan for his third try of the match. Sullivan again kicked the goal and we had won a sensational Test 18-13 after being 0-9 down.

You could fill a book with the memories of that Final Test - it will always remain, to me, my First Test - but I shall just confine myself to one - of the character on the famous Sydney Hill who shouted, when a lot of us flung up our arms and appealed for a penalty kick, 'Wait till George Duckworth hears about youse blokes!' Perhaps it was the same fellow who let all and sundry know after I had scored a cheeky blind-side try against New South Wales that I was 'a pommie b----------'.

Many people described the 1932 touring party as the best ever, and some people say it has not been equalled since. It is perhaps true to say that the accepted first team would have had a hard task to beat the 'ham and eggers', as we call the thirteen who are normally reserved for the country games - I was one of them in 1932.

Jim Sullivan was a magnificent captain and a real inspiration to the team. And you cannot forget Joe Thompson, the front-row forward with legs like oak trees, or Juicy Adams, the will-o'-the-wisp scrum-half, or Stan Smith, who could run like a greyhound.

Yes, a magnificent touring party. It won two and lost one

of the Tests, and of the other matches, thirteen were won, one lost and one drawn.

Rugby Renegade

17

AUSTRALIA: PART TWO

My international career was now coming on apace. After my return from the Australian tour of 1932 I won further caps for Wales and also played in the three Test matches when Australia visited England during the 1933-4 season. We won all three.

Then came 1936, and another tour to Australia, and once again I was selected, this time as one of the centre three-quarters. Four of my Salford colleagues also made the trip - wingmen Barney Hudson and Alan Edwards, and the terrible half-back twins of Emlyn Jenkins and Billy Watkins.

I felt much more confident going on my second trip. Not only did I know what to expect, but I had had four more years' experience in the game and had much more confidence in myself.

It was great, too, renewing old friendships in Australia, for, believe me, although many of the games on these tours are tough, firm friendships are made. The Australians are most hospitable, and they go out of their way to make any touring party welcome. They even entertained us in their own homes.

When we arrived we discovered that the Australian critics had decided we were a formidable combination, and the forecasts were that we would hand out some pretty hefty defeats. So it was not surprising that well over fifty thousand people thronged the Sydney Cricket Ground to see us perform in the first match of the tour against Sydney - and that on a dull, grey, foggy day, too.

And the huge crowd got a shock. Instead of the runaway victory, we were often struggling before we won 15-13, thanks to a late goal by Martin Hodgson, who booted one over the bar from the half-way line. But the thing that everyone noticed was that we scored but one try - Hodgson and I shared six goals equally - whereas the Sydney boys crossed our line three times.

The Aussies began to think we were vulnerable. And they thought so even more when New South Wales, with a man injured, beat us 18-14 before another fifty thousand crowd on the Sydney Cricket Ground. This certainly was a shaky start.

Then came the real shock - a 21-16 defeat by Newcastle before a record crowd. What a start to a tour!

The all-important First Test match was looming up, and we had a painfully long injury list. A number of players were doubtful and Barney Hudson was definitely out of the side. My chances of playing were slim because of an ankle injury. When the team was finally announced there was no Risman and no Hudson.

The crowd was well over sixty thousand, and at one time it seemed that our weakened side would hold the Aussies, and at half-time we were just one point behind - two penalty goals to a try. But in the second half they gave us a thrashing, and before we knew where we were, we were down by no less than 24-3. Alan Edwards made a late try for Beverley, which Hodgson converted, but we had lost the First Test badly. What is more, we had lost two games in succession!

We were all determined to show the Aussies we were not going to make them a present of the Ashes, although a number of their newspapermen, who had forecast woeful tidings for their men when we arrived, were now saying that the Ashes were as good as out of Britain. Even the fact that we won quite a few matches after the debacle in the opening Test did not shatter their optimism, but we were quite confident when we reached Brisbane for the Second Test. We were determined to win because we knew that a defeat would ruin the rest of the trip.

Happily enough we were able to field our strongest side, and this included four of the Salford contingent - Alan Edwards and myself as partners in the three-quarter line, and Emlyn Jenkins and Billy Watkins as partners at half-back.

The stadium was packed, despite the rain, and probably most Australians hoped that their men would clinch the rubber by a victory. But they reckoned without Tommy Armitt, our hooker, who was in magnificent form. There were seventy-five scrums... and Tommy gained possession from forty-eight of them. That was just what we wanted, and with half-backs like Jenkins and Watkins we were able to use that valuable possession. Our backs had a great time of it.

We took the lead after about ten minutes when Edwards burst over for a try, and then I kicked a penalty goal for my first-ever score in a Test match. Australia hit back with an amazing try by Archie Crippen, who was making his first Test appearance at the age of twenty. He snapped up the ball right behind me and set off on one of the most thrilling dashes anyone could wish to see. Fully seventy yards he raced before touching down, sending the crowd mad with delight. The try was converted, so it was five-all at half-time.

After the break, Alan Edwards turned up with another try in the corner, which I converted, so we were off to a five-point lead again, and a penalty goal to each side after that gave us a 12-7 victory and squared the rubber at one game each.

And so to the greatest day of all, Saturday, July 18, 1936, a particularly great day for me because I was made captain, the first time I had led a Test match side. And as I walked on to the field at the Sydney Cricket Ground in front of sixty thousand spectators, I felt particularly proud because four of my club colleagues - Barney Hudson, Alan Edwards, Emlyn Jenkins and Billy Watkins - were following me. In fact the only non-Salford player in the three-quarter line was Stan Brogden, who played right centre, with me inside with him. Edwards was on the left wing, with Hudson on the right.

Barney scored one of our tries - Brogden getting the other - and with Martin Hodgson converting both tries and also kicking a penalty, I was able to lead my men to victory by the same score as in the Second Test - 12-7.

There was no prouder man in the whole of Australia that day than Augustus John Risman, when I received the magnificent Courtney Trophy at the end of the game on behalf of the Great Britain team.

But even the proud memory of being captain of a victorious Test team fades when I think of that match we played in New Zealand against South Island at Christchurch. The Rugby Union people had organised a rival game at a ground just half a mile from that on which our game would have been played, but it seemed that the weather was to intervene in any Rugby League - Rugby Union war because it snowed throughout the night before the big day, and on the morning of the match there was four inches of snow on the ground.

The Rugby Union game was postponed, but the League

people were determined to carry on. And oh, what a game it was!

One half of the ground had been cleared, but the other half was covered in freezing snow and sleet. It was sheer murder to play on that surface, and I felt so cold that I thought I was going to die. Whenever we moved we could feel our boots cutting through the ice and squelching in the water underneath.

I was emergency scrum-half and I became so sick and ill with it that I could hardly feel the ball when I handled it, and once when I was putting the ball into the scrum I collapsed. I remember absolutely nothing about it. I can recall bending down to put the ball into the scrum, and the next thing I remember is waking up in the snow and ice that was piled high around the touchlines.

The trainers told me that I had collapsed face downwards into the ice, snow and slush, and when I came round they were trying to revive me with sips of brandy. Eventually the blood in my veins thawed and I was able to go back on to the field for the last ten minutes.

The dressing accommodation was not wonderful at Christchurch, so immediately after the game we were bundled into the taxis - yes, still wearing our frozen, muddy kit - and rushed to our hotel. I was sharing a room with Emlyn Jenkins, and we both had the same idea immediately we got into our room. We filled the bath with steaming hot water and leapt into it - the pair of us still wearing our football kit, including boots.

We both lay there and soaked for half an hour. It was heaven after a hell!

Rugby Renegade

18

AUSTRALIA: PART THREE

The war brought to an end all thoughts of Rugby League tours abroad, and it was not until 1946 the that Rugby League was able to visit Australia once again. Even then it was a most difficult operation. In fact the problems were such that no one could have blamed the Rugby League Council if it had decided that it could not possibly raise a touring party of twenty-six players and transport it to the other end of the earth. But the members of the Council felt that it was essential that, with the war just over, the friendship between the Mother Country and the great Dominion of Australia should be resumed in the game. They believed, quite rightly, that the public had a large appetite for sport and that a tour at this difficult time would be such a success that it would be well worth all the hard work it entailed.

The greatest difficulty was getting the party out to Australia. The end of the war meant that thousands of troops had to be taken to their homes, and most of the world's transport was geared for war purposes, not for taking footballers thousands of miles from Britain to Australia.

That, the biggest problem of all, was solved, and I have never been impertinent enough to enquire how! For, believe it or not, we were booked to travel on the Aircraft Carrier Indomitable. Now getting a Rugby League party on to an aircraft carrier was something, and whoever was responsible for it is herewith handed all the congratulation in the world. For without Indomitable there could have been no tour.

And what a voyage it was! Indomitable sailed from Plymouth, full of Australians and New Zealanders who were going home after their magnificent service in Europe. Maybe the fact that we travelled on a warship that was being used as a transport would give you the idea that it was not a comfortable trip, but don't you believe it. My two previous tours were in luxury liners, but the trip in Indomitable was easily the best I have had. It was an experience I would not have missed for anything.

The whole Rugby League party was put on the crew list as Petty Officers, we were made members of the Petty Officers' mess, and given all the privileges of Petty Officers.

As you can imagine, sleeping accommodation was a wee bit tight, but I - probably because I was skipper of the party - was allocated a bunk in the chart-room, which was amidships. Others were not quite so lucky. Their bunks were near the engine-room, and they spent each night simply bathed in perspiration. One of the unlucky ones was our big forward Frank Whitcombe, and we lost no opportunity of telling Frank that his nightly Turkish bath helped to keep his weight in check! Fortunately, perhaps, for Frank, the trip was the shortest of the three I have made to Australia. It took us just four weeks to get from Plymouth to Fremantle. Maybe if it had taken any longer Frank would have lost so much weight he would have been a candidate for one of the half-back positions!

Travelling on an aircraft carrier gave us wonderful facilities for training, for we were able to use the huge flight decks, which were some hundred and fifty yards long. That meant we could sprint, practice moves and do just about every type of training possible on shore. That, together with the splendid spirit of friendship which existed throughout the ship, and the thrill of calling at such ports as Malta, Aden and Colombo, meant that by the time we arrived in Fremantle we were easily the fittest Rugby League team that had ever landed in Australia.

We all thought that the Indomitable was going to continue its journey to Melbourne and that we were going with it, but the Captain received orders to turn round at Fremantle, so we were stranded. We were put into a Transit Camp in Fremantle and had to remain there for a week until alternative transport to Melbourne could be found. We played a couple of trial matches during our stay, and then came the news that we were on our way - to Melbourne by troop train.

This was one of the greatest experiences of my life. It took four days to cross the vast continent of Australia, and never once during the whole trip did we take off our clothes. We stood, sat and slept in the same garments, although to say we slept is a spot of exaggeration. There were, of course, no sleeping berths, so we had to rest where and how we could - on the floor, on the seat, on the luggage rack or even in the corridor.

No food was provided on the train, but at meal-times the train would stop at various points en route and we would dive out of the carriages, armed with the good old service 'irons' (knife, fork, spoon and plate) and line up at the cafeteria, where piles of stew would be poured on to our plates. We just sat on the ground and ate - and fought like mad to keep off the millions of flies!

At each stop, aborigines would come to greet us, and we began to get quite friendly with them. They seemed to appear out of nowhere, for the great desert in the middle of Australia looks absolutely uninhabited.

We had no training during our four days on the train, for it was a luxury to be able to move, let alone do any physical exercise. Sometimes the train would slow down, and when it did some of us would jump down and trot alongside it. Once the train picked up speed without any warning, and Frank Whitcombe just managed to grab the last rail of the last coach. If he had failed, one of our star forwards would have been left all on his lonesome in the Australian desert!

By the time we arrived in Melbourne we must have been the most unfit Rugby League side ever to arrive in that famous city - and we still faced another train journey to Sydney!

Fortunately a compartment had been reserved for us, which pleased us all - until we discovered that the reservation had been made for thirteen players only! There were twenty-six of us (two full teams), plus a couple of managers!

There was nothing else for it but to pile into the cramped space - twenty-eight people in the space reserved for thirteen - and when we arrived in Sydney we were still wearing the same clothes we had worn when we had left Fremantle. We must have looked the most disreputable Rugby League side ever to arrive in Sydney!

We had been transformed, then, from the fittest to the unfittest and then to the most disreputable-looking side, all in the space of a week!

Some of the newspapers tried to whip up a scare story about our trip. They claimed that we were near to open rebellion and that we moaned so much that we were barred from speaking to reporters.

That is absolute nonsense. No one is going to claim that we loved our trip from Fremantle to Sydney - who would have done? - but the 1946 party was composed of a grand bunch of lads who realised that the tour was being made under extreme difficulties and that everyone was doing his or her best. So there were no grumbles, and no group of sportsmen has ever been further away from rebellion - open or covert.

I will go further and say that the 1946 tour was the happiest I made. No one could have wished for finer fellows or for a finer spirit to exist in a team. The experiences we had, although tough at times, often raised laughs later, and they served the more-than-useful purpose of binding the fellows together into one big happy family.

This, no doubt, annoyed some of the newspaper reporters, who were aching to get a scandal story. That is why they tried to sell the idea that we were riddled with dissension, when the exact opposite was the truth.

For instance, I had a great pal in Sydney called Sam Peters, and he visited Brisbane when we were playing in that city. He didn't stay at the same hotel as us tourists, but he asked me if I would like to pop along to his hotel one morning for breakfast. I did, and took Jack Kitching with me. Sam's hotel was only fifty yards from ours, and while we were breakfasting one of the reporters saw us.

Out came the story - Risman and Kitching are not staying with their colleagues!

There were other such scare stories, and although they were untrue they had an unsettling effect on the whole party. After all, nobody likes to read such stories even though they have no foundation, and the only time the boys really got annoyed was when these stories - pure inventions - appeared.

Rugby Renegade

One journalist in particular was responsible for the majority of these stories, and we were convinced that the idea was to spread discontent through the happiest party that had ever visited Australia. So we decided to call a meeting of the whole touring party - players and managers. We all promised not take the slightest notice of anything that appeared in the newspapers. From that moment onwards we decided to treat such stories as a joke, Frank Whitcombe adding the rider that he would be perfectly willing to assume the responsibility of throwing that particular reporter down the back stairs of the Daniel Hotel any time it was convenient!

We decided it would be better not to accept Frank's kind offer.

Frank Whitcombe was the great comic of the party. He kept us all in the very best of humour, even in the difficult times - and there are always difficult times on any tour - and he was a magnificent team man, the sort of man on and off the field that is indispensable to any touring party.

The first match of the tour was at Junee against the Southern Districts, and although we won easily enough 36-4, we did have some trouble with the interpretation of the laws. The referee penalised a forward pass as offside - that is, he awarded a free kick - and it was through this that I was nearly sent off, a fate which, thank goodness, was never mine throughout the whole of my career. We were penalised time after time so I had a word with the referee and suggested that something should be done about this interpretation of the rule. His reply was that if he had any more trouble with me I would go off the field!

But despite small spots of misunderstanding like that - and what touring party in any sport does not have them? - it was a tremendously happy tour. Never have I known such hospitality. The Australians are famous for the welcome they give to visitors, but they really surpassed themselves in 1946. There was bunting everywhere, we were invited into people's homes, and never has a visiting team had such kindness lavished on it.

In Canberra we were presented to the Governor-General, then His Royal Highness the Duke of Gloucester, and we also had a most happy meeting with Mr. Chifley, the Prime Minister. We met him in the Houses of Parliament, and he spoke to each member of the team as if they were personal friends of his.

We were allowed to use all the clubs, and we took full advantage of the facilities and welcome accorded to us at Tattersall's Club in Sydney, where there is a swimming-pool and a masseur.

History was made on the tour when some of us travelled by air. We travelled North for a game by train but returned by air, and never before had a Rugby League touring party travelled by aircraft.

At the other end of the scale, one journey was by goods train. Our passenger coach was attached to the goods train, which was carrying cows, pigs and sheep. And what a noise those animals made!

Naturally, our goods train did not travel as fast as the normal passenger trains, so a journey that normally took anything from sixteen to twenty-four hours took us forty-eight!

Australian trains do not carry dining-cars. Instead, the train stops and you take your meal in the refreshment room of the station. Wherever we stopped, we were besieged by well-wishers who were so keen on shaking our hands that they hardly gave us any time to eat!

Our first big game was against New South Wales on the Sydney Cricket Ground and it looked as if we were in for a defeat when the State side ran up a 10-0 lead early in the second half. Against us in that match, which was watched by over fifty thousand people, were two forwards now very well known in England - Arthur Clues and Harry Bath - but Bath had the misfortune to sprain his knee after only twenty minutes' play and he was a passenger for the rest of the game.

Nevertheless, even against twelve fit men it looked as if we were in for a defeat. But Ike Owens went over for a try made by Tommy McCue, who had a magnificent game, though all the Australians claim that Owens knocked-on before he went over. But the referee gave a try, and as I kicked the goal we were only down 5-10. Then followed a couple of penalty goals to make it 9-10, and Eric Batten put us into the lead with a try near the end. I kicked the goal, although the newspapermen, who often think they are better placed in the stand than the touch-judge behind the goal, said the ball went wide.

How often these newspapermen are wrong, yet sometimes right. They made a fuss about my goal and the try by Owens, and then along came Pat Devery, the New South Wales half-back, to say that Owens did not knock-on. 'I knocked the ball over the line,' he said. So that was a try all right. But the goal? Well, a movie camera showed the ball had passed a foot wide. Still it counted.

In the return match we won easily enough by 21-7, even though the selection of the team was a difficult job because of injuries. As this game took place just before the First Test match, we felt awfully happy at the result .... especially as seven of the New South Wales team were chosen for the Test. We drew that First Test 8-8, but we won the Second in Brisbane and swamped Australia in the Third Test at Sydney. So we became the first touring party ever to remain undefeated in a Test series in Australia. Not only that, we retained the Ashes, as we had done in every previous Test series in which I had taken part.

On this 1946 tour we found that the standard of football in Australia varied a great deal. The general standard was good, but the standard in some of the country districts was very low indeed. The reason for this was that the game was probably not played often during the war when so many of the best players were away.

In one of the country districts at Mackay we won by a runaway score and had almost a hundred points on the board. At the final whistle we were just three short, and during the game Jimmy Lewthwaite set up a personal record with seven tries, and Ernest Ward kicked fifteen goals!

Yet at the other end of the scale, we were beaten at Woollongong, a result that was comparable to, say, Doncaster, at the present time, beating a touring side. Woollongong had a wonderful forward called Tiny Russell - he got that nickname because he weighed something between sixteen and seventeen stones! - and he made mincemeat of us. He was simply terrific, bouncing us all over the place.

Perhaps our most exciting game was against Queensland, who were leading us by just one point - 25-24 - when I had the chance to give us victory with the last kick of the match. It was, I admit, a tremendous strain taking that goal kick, but the position was an easy one and I am sure everyone on the ground would have put his shirt on my sending the ball over the bar and between the posts. But football is a funny game and footballers are funny people. I missed ... and we lost!

One trip I shall never forget was the one to Rockhampton, a lovely country town. But this lovely country town had been besieged by American troops during the war, many of the hotels had been taken over and there had not been enough time to get the place shipshape again.

We were accommodated in two hotels, and I was shocked to find that my room had the wallpaper hanging in strips from the walls, the bed was rickety and the sheets were in shreds. There was nothing for it but to make the best of it, so I crawled into bed. But within a couple of minutes I heard a lot of shouting. I rushed out into the corridor to see what the trouble was, and discovered that Eric Batten had lifted up a seat and found it alive with bugs. Then there was a terrific crash upstairs. That was caused by Frank Whitcombe. He had been given a bed in a corridor, and the bed was so rickety that he had gone right though it - all seventeen stones of him!

Fortunately for our peace of mind, we were all moved the next morning to another hotel!

The Australian is a born gambler, but on no other tour did I see the amount of gambling that took place in 1946. I attended several Sunday games, and Australian 'fivers' were being thrown about like pieces of paper on bets like 'Who'll win the next scrum?' - 'Bet he gains more than forty yards on this next kick to touch' - 'So-and-so will score before so-and-so' - 'Lay odds on this kick at goal'.

Heavy money went on the results of matches. But the *piece de resistance* as far as I was concerned happened right at the end of the tour. I was actually offered £500 by a character to make sure that Great Britain did not win the Final Test at Sydney. Needless to say, the offer was turned down flat, and I used the incident in a dressing-room pep-talk before the game. The boys went out rarin' to go. Bribery to make the British team lose a rugby match? A thing unheard of, and I know every British player that day would sooner have died than lose.

The score was decisive. Great Britain 20, Australia 7. I got three goals!

We made history again when we went from Australia to New Zealand by air. Normally it was a four days' boat journey, but our team were in Auckland within eight hours of leaving Rose Bay, Sydney.

We may have been forgiven for regarding the New Zealand trip as a holiday following the rigours of the Australian tour. The waters and baths of Rotorua were sampled in a three days' stay there. Here I was prompted by the rest of the team to concoct a letter to the Rugby League Council asking for compensation of £10 a man for clothes ruined on the train trip across the Nullaboor Plain. We got an immediate refusal.

New Zealand hospitality was lavished upon us, with numerous food parcels being sent home to our families by considerate food firms.

Only one Test was played, and we were left with a profound respect for Kiwi Rugby League. They beat us 13-8. We scored two tries and one goal, New Zealand got one try and five goals.

We left New Zealand on the Rangitiki, the 'Brides' Boat', carrying the wives and families of American and Canadian servicemen who had been stationed in New Zealand.

Yes, the 1946 tour was fun. We had our discomforts, we had our laughs and we had some rip-roaring games of football, most of which ended in our favour. Our team spirit could not have been better, and there wasn't a player in the party who did not thoroughly enjoy himself.

The people themselves were magnificent, and although it is hard to mention names when so many people showered us within kindness, I could not ignore the work of Lady Violet Braddon, the wife of Sir Henry Braddon. She went out of her way to help us in Sydney. She fixed up entertainments for us, she arranged visits for us to private houses, and she did just about everything to make us feel comfortable and welcome.

It was the actions of people like Lady Braddon which made us all remember the 1946 tour with nothing but happiness.

Thanks, Australia, for a wonderful time.

Rugby Renegade

19

IT'S A PART-TIME JOB

Rugby League allows professionalism - although there are more amateur players than professional players - but there are no full-time Rugby League players as there are full-time Association Football players. That is to say that in Rugby League the actual football is a paid hobby. During the week all the players have jobs to do, and I insist that all my young players put their jobs before their football.

That is not to say that I agree with them neglecting their training. Far from it. The training schedule of a Rugby League team is rigorous because Rugby League is a strenuous game which can only be played by men who are one hundred per cent fit.

Training takes place on two nights a week, and most grounds have small floodlighting systems which are good enough for training but not for match play. The players report to the ground at six o'clock - straight after their work - and do a three hours' stint. These three-hour training sessions consist of sprinting, tactics (both theory and practical), general practice, massage and team talks. If there are any mid-week games - and Rugby League seems to have a lot of them! - then I insist that players train two nights before the match. Otherwise training nights are Tuesday and Thursday.

Comparing that training schedule with the schedules which are in force at the first-class Association Football clubs would lead one to believe that the Rugby League players do not get enough training, but in actual practice that is not true. The Rugby League players do train enough, and they have proved time and time again that their stamina is far superior to that of the average Association Football player. If you asked a Rugby League team to go on to the field with soccer players in any set of conditions and play either eighty minutes of rugby or ninety minutes of soccer, the Rugby League players would last the pace far better than their opponents.

This is because Rugby League training is better organised. The players have just six hours a week and they don't waste a minute. They put everything they know into their training with the result that all our training time is efficiently used. It isn't in soccer.

Nor do the Rugby League players lose anything by working during the day. The game could not afford the luxury of full-time professionals, and even if it could I would not agree with the system. A man's first consideration must be his job because football is too precarious an occupation. At the very best a career in football is a short one, and, at the worst, injuries can end a career much earlier than expected.

If a player is happy and contented in his job he will be happy and contented in his football. He will have no financial worries and he will be able to put his heart and soul into his training and into his match play. Certainly the player in full employment is better off than the player who relies solely on his football for a living.

It is true, of course, that Rugby League players have tough jobs. Many of them work down the pits, others are steel workers or engineers, and the majority of them do what is termed officially as 'heavy work'. But this does not harm them - who was it who said that hard work never killed anyone? On the contrary it does them the world of good. It toughens them up, builds up their muscles and helps to keep them fit. It does not, as some people have claimed, tire them out.

Rugby League clubs rarely have strict rules about drinking and smoking either. We trust our players and few of them let us down. They are keen and determined and know that if they ruin their health they will soon find themselves out of the side - and that, in Rugby League, means a financial loss, as I shall explain elsewhere.

The players know that too much smoking will affect their breathing and that it is not good for them to drink a lot during the middle of the week. And the players are not prepared to do anything that will affect their football.

If, of course, we do find a player who follows a steady course of drinking throughout the week, then we know full well that his form will suffer and that he will have to lose his place in the side. And no Rugby League player likes that.

In short, then, we treat our players like men, and they behave like men.

I have already admitted that Rugby League is a strenuous game. I will even admit that it is a tough and rigorous game. But I will never admit that it is a 'dirty' game.

Much has been said and written about Rugby League being 'dirty', but most of this is just wild talk. No one expects rugby to be played by namby-pambies or by girls. It is a man's game, meant to be played by men who can give and take knocks without crying. The players are made as fit as possible in their training sessions, and they are trained to withstand bumps and take bruises.

The most common injuries which they suffer are strained and pulled muscles. Perhaps the most prevalent injury of the lot is the shoulder injury, for the very nature of the game makes bruised and dislocated shoulders all too common.

Many of these injuries are caused by the ground conditions, and there are people who believe that we should change the time of the season. Lance Todd, for instance, was a strong advocate of summer football, but I never agreed with him. I still don't. There is nothing worse for Rugby League football than a hard ground, and we have enough of those at the beginning and the end of the season as it is. If we played during the summer the grounds would be harder still and there would be more injuries. Wasn't it in 1948 that a dreadful winter caused the extension of the football season, which went on until the end of June or the beginning of July? Believe me, it was murder playing on those hard grounds.

So don't kid yourself that the injuries that occur in Rugby League are caused by 'dirty' play. They are not. What is more, the injury rate in Rugby League is lower than it is in soccer!

There are, of course, some Rugby League players who are 'dirty' and who will try to cheat the rules. But they are in the minority. The majority are tough, but they are not 'dirty'. True, in any sport of bodily contact, men momentarily lose their tempers, but these tempers soon cool down, and it is a fact that tempers are lost now and then at soccer, Rugby Union or any other similar sport.

I will go further in defending Rugby League against the charge that it is a 'dirty' game and say that generally speaking Rugby League is cleaner than Rugby Union. I have played Rugby Union and I have watched it often, and I have seen things go unpunished on a Rugby Union field that would warrant marching orders and a six-match suspension in Rugby League. Many of the things that go on in the Rugby Union loose scrums - and even in the set scrums - would never be tolerated in Rugby League.

Let it never be forgotten that Rugby League is the strictest of all sports, which explains why more of our players are sent off the field. Our referees have been told to be tough with any law breakers, and no Rugby League player gets away with offences as easily as the Rugby Union player or the soccer player.

We do not just content ourselves with handing out punishments for 'dirty' play. We send players off for breaches of the rules like putting the ball into the scrum. Our view is that every man in the first-class Rugby League world is a highly skilled player and should know the rules and be able to obey them. If anyone breaks those rules then he must go off the field and be punished with a suspension.

So, if half-backs persist in not putting the ball into the scrum properly, if hookers strike for the ball before it has entered the scrum, or if any player continually breaks a rule, even though he is not guilty of 'dirty' play, he is sent off. And quite rightly so, too.

But do Rugby Union half-backs get sent off for not putting the ball into the scrum correctly? Do Rugby Union players get sent off if they do not release the ball immediately they are tackled? Of course they don't, but they would if they played in Rugby League.

And we would send off soccer players who are guilty of a foul throw-in. During their period of suspension they would be able to practice taking throw-ins!

Nor do we allow any arguments with the referee. All our players are told that the referee's decision, right or wrong, is final, and any man who disputes that decision gets his marching orders.

And when Rugby League players are sent off the field they are severely punished by the Disciplinary Committee. Suspensions are heavy and many a player has found himself banned for six matches, with a consequent loss of pay.

We insist on clean play and discipline, and if anyone wants to transgress that code then he can do so at his own risk and take the punishment.

So forget this nonsense about Rugby League being a 'dirty' game. It is cleaner than either of the other football codes, it is much more disciplined, its referees are more severe, and so is its Disciplinary Committee.

20

FINANCE AND RUGBY LEAGUE

The thought of men being paid to play football is abhorrent to some people, although why anyone should be expected to entertain the paying public without receiving any financial reward is beyond me. The common argument against professionalism is that the commercialism in the game has now become much more important than the sport.

Which is absolute nonsense. True, the professional players get paid - openly and legally, unlike some amateurs! But that in no way interferes with their love of the sport. If a player loves the game, he will love it whether he gets paid or not. I have played Rugby Union as an amateur and Rugby League as a professional, and I have enjoyed every minute of my time in both codes. The mere fact that I played Rugby League as a professional for money did not affect my enjoyment of the game one little bit. After all, there is no greater feeling than having a hand in a good movement.

Maybe there are exceptions to that rule, but then there are exceptions to every rule. I would not attempt to deny that there are some professionals who think only of the money, but believe me, they are in a tiny minority. Generally speaking, you will find the professional sportsman the most generous of men, always willing to help any worthy cause.

But Rugby League is a professional game attracting paying customers, and the professional player is entitled to some reward for his services, just like the professional doctor, the professional entertainer, or the professional salesman. Every Rugby League player is on a part-time contract, so his earnings from football are over and above those he gets from his regular job.

The payments made in Rugby League are not covered by any rule. The scale of payments is purely a matter to be decided between the clubs, acting as the employers, and the players, acting as the employees, and I am not in a position to give any facts about how much players receive with any other club except my own, Salford.

I am a firm believer in every man in the team receiving the same money. Football is a team game, and the success of any player depends upon the co-operation he receives from his colleagues. So it is not fair to pay one player more than another. Some clubs, I know, do not agree with that view, and there are clubs which make private arrangements with each individual.

Where there is a difference it is in the size of the signing-on fee. Star Rugby Union players have commanded figures of anything up to the £6,000 Leeds paid for Lewis Jones, and this payment compares favourably with the signing-on fees offered by Italian soccer clubs, where the fee is paid over a period and is subject to taxation.

Not every player, of course, receives so much. Six thousand pounds is a fantastic fee only paid to real star men, and there are few of that category around. More often than not the signing-on fee is much smaller, and it can well be under £100 for a beginner. Often it is. The rules of the Rugby League state quite clearly that no player may receive more than one signing-on fee, so there is no question of a star man receiving £6,000 for two years and then another £6,000 after he has fulfilled that contract.

Still, these star men are one up on their soccer counterparts, who only receive a very small signing-on fee (can I say 'officially'?) on their initial signing by a club. I once travelled on the same train as a famous soccer team, and, chatting to the trainer, an old friend, I saw the eyes of some famous players open wide at the mention of the signing fees obtained in the Rugby League game. 'All for themselves?' they gasped, and could hardly believe it when I said 'Yes'!

But unlike the Association Football player, a Rugby League player does not receive a weekly wage. He just receives a match fee, and if he does not play, then he does not get paid. This might, at first glance, seem hard, but one has to remember that Rugby League is not such a wealthy game as its friendly rival, and few of the clubs could afford to pay their players a weekly wage whether they play in the first team or not.

At Salford we pay our players a minimum of £4 10s. a match. They receive that, the lowest possible figure, if they get beaten. If they win they receive £9 10s. A draw away from home is classed as a win, a draw at home is classed as a defeat.

Other clubs have other systems. Leeds announced, for instance, that they were going to pay their players a flat £10 for a win, home or away, and Oldham a few seasons ago offered their players a complicated bonus system which meant that the bonus would increase by 10s. with each succeeding win. The scheme proved highly successful for the players but highly expensive for the club - the team won game after game without a break!

Rugby Renegade

There are times, providing the club can afford it, when the bonus money is increased for an important game. For instance, if we were playing Oldham, one of the top teams, in an important match, we could offer our players a special bonus for winning. I have heard all sorts of stories about these special bonuses, and it is said that in some important matches the players can be on £100 for a win. Simple economics will show you how rarely, if ever, that figure is offered, for not many Rugby League games provide gate receipts of £1,300.

When Workington Town went to Wembley and won the Rugby League Challenge Cup, the players were offered what we thought were fair bonuses. For the victory in the first round they were given £5, £10 for the second round, £30 for the semi-final and £50 for the Cup Final itself. These bonuses were paid as extras to the match fees and ordinary win bonuses.

What happens, you may ask, if a player is injured and is prevented from being considered for selection? To cover such unfortunate cases we have a special insurance scheme, and in addition to his National Health Insurance money (if the player is prevented from working), this insurance scheme at Salford ensures that each injured player will receive £4 each week.

It may be interesting at this point to compare the present rates of pay in force at Salford with the pay we received during the club's heyday. Today the players receive £9 10s. for a win, or a draw away from home, and £4 10s. for a defeat, or a home draw. In 1937, we Salford players received £3 if we won either home or away or drew away from home, and just 35s. if we were beaten or if we drew on our own ground. So the rates of pay at Salford have been trebled.

To pay the present fees, we at Salford need an average home gate of six thousand people if we are to break even -

and that leaves nothing in the kitty for new players or for ground improvements. As our gates hardly average that, we have to depend upon the Football Pool for any extras.

Unlike the Football League, the Rugby League does not lay down any specific talent money payments for a team finishing in the top four of the league, but the players at Salford have been told that they will receive an end-of-the-season payment depending on the season's results. If they finish in the top four of the league the players will share £500. This is an incentive bonus which the directors have agreed to introduce now that Entertainments Tax has been abolished. I think it represents a real effort to encourage the players.

In addition, the players have been offered a shilling each for every try that is scored, which should encourage them to go on fighting for points even when a game is obviously won or lost.

There will, of course, be those who say that we should increase those bonuses, but with our present income and our present staff - we have forty-five players on our books, five fewer than the maximum allowed by Rugby League rules - these bonuses and talent money represent the maximum the club can pay. Should the gate improve, then the money will be passed on to the players.

Rugby Renegade

21

THE SPECTATOR

My experience of sporting spectators covers a wide variety
of sports, but I can say with all honesty that the Rugby
League spectator has a more profound knowledge of the
game than the spectator of any other sport. More than that -
the Rugby League supporter often knows as much about the
game as the average player, and in few, if any, sports can you
say that.

Oh, yes, I know we have our bad spectators, the sort of
people who hurl abuse from the terraces and from the stand,
but every sport has people like that, and in Rugby League
we have fewer of them to worry about than most other
sports.

The barracker, the man who loves to shout abuse can,
and should, be dealt with through the club programme; on
top of that, any good manager will tell his players not to take
the slightest notice of the barracker. Actually, the Rugby
League player is more fortunate than his colleagues who
play Rugby Union or Association Football, for in Rugby

Rugby Renegade

League the player is in the game far more than he is in either of those other two sports, and he has, therefore, less chance of hearing any abuse that might be flung from the crowd.

One time the players do hear the crowd, though, is when there is a concerted roar of encouragement. There is nothing more certain to spur players on to greater efforts than the tremendous roar of a crowd which is right behind you. If you are attacking your opponents' line and your spectators make a fearful din as they cheer you on, those cheers bring extra strength to your already tired legs, and encourage you to try just that little bit harder - even though you might already be giving all you have!

Conversely, the defenders are made nervous. They know that the crowd is roaring for the attacking side, and when you are defending under conditions like that you feel that everyone is against you. That is when you are more liable to make that mistake which could lead to a try being scored against you.

Generally speaking, the behaviour of the spectators at Rugby League matches is excellent, but, as always, there are exceptions. There are times when there are lapses, when spectators get beyond themselves in their enthusiasm for one particular club. In all sports there are cases of spectators being so upset when their favourites are beaten that they go off the rails and behave as they shouldn't behave. Fortunately, those occasions are less prevalent in the Rugby League than in any similar sport, and they are less prevalent because everyone in Rugby League is brought up to accept defeat in the same spirit as he accepts victory, and everyone knows full well that the referee's decision is the only one that counts. Therefore, Rugby League supporters know full well that it is no use screaming abuse at a referee who has given a decision, and it is no use being stupid, childish and silly and waiting for the referee to leave the ground so that you can howl abuse at him.

Many of the indiscretions are committed on the spur of the moment, and clubs could help considerably by making sure that none of the spectators can interfere with any of the players and officials as they walk between the dressing-room and the field. If the players and officials have to walk through spectators at the end of the match it is asking for trouble, for that is the time when passions are still running high, when tempers have not had the chance to cool down. A spectator might say or do something at that time that he would regret later and which would bring a heap of trouble on to the club's shoulders.

Take the case of Charlie Appleton, the Test and Cup Finals referee. After a match in which Salford were concerned, genial Charlie had to struggle with an irate spectator who accused Mr. Appleton of giving the Salford players advice during the game. Salford forward Eric Ayles had to do a rescue act. 'And I was only telling Salford to get a move on with a kick at goal!' Charlie explained!

Mind you, there are characters in Rugby League just as there are characters in any other sport, and it would be a great pity if we were to lose them - characters like the woman with the St. Helens Umbrella.

This lady was a fervent supporter of St. Helens, and at each match she would take up her favourite position- just by the players' entrance to the field. Always she would bring her umbrella, although no matter how hard it rained she would never use it for the purpose umbrellas were invented. All she wanted it for was to crack it across the heads of the visiting players each time they came on or off the field.

She became the talk of the whole of Rugby League. When the visitors arrived at the St. Helens ground, the St. Helens players would pull their legs about the welcome they were going to get. As the players left their dressing-room, the captain always gave the same advice: 'All right, lads, here it comes. Make it snappy as you go through that tunnel or else she'll beat your brains out.'

The same advice was given as the players left the field for half-time and at the end of the match. And it was necessary.

But the St. Helens lady was not vicious. She was just an enthusiastic Saints supporter who thought she was doing her bit for her team by cracking some of the opposing players across the head! She just hit out indiscriminately - I never heard of her making a dead set against any one player - and we players would be upset if we didn't get the crack as we ran out!

She was just a lovable character, a real enthusiast, and even though her enthusiasm probably did go off the rails when she saw the opponents, she was harmless, and secretly we all loved her.

Mind you, no one in the game would want the idea of the St. Helens Umbrella to spread. One is enough!

22

DEAR JUNIOR —

You can call this chapter an open letter to all the youngsters, to all those who want to make a career of this game of rugby, or who just want to play it for fun.

Rugby is a great game, a game that calls for energy, for nerve, for skill and for enthusiasm. If you haven't got all those four qualities, then look elsewhere for your sport. Rugby is not the game for you.

It is not, as some people think, an easy game to play, a game in which you only have to chase around the field like a madman and have the time of your life pulling opponents to the ground. There is much more to rugby than that. You have to learn to tackle properly, to position yourself, to catch the ball (not as easy as it looks), to pass the ball (much harder than it looks) and kick the ball.

Take the tackle first. You can, if you like, make a grab at the collar of the jersey of an opponent, but you must not expect that sort of a tackle to stop anyone. More often than not the man with the ball is running, and this gives him extra momentum. Grabbing his collar to stop him will be just as effective as grabbing the handrail in an effort to stop a bus that is moving away from the stop.

The one way to tackle is to get your man low, and the old adage that 'the bigger they are the harder they fall' will then always work. No man, however clever, can run without his legs, and if you grab him low round the legs or waist you will have tackled him.

Positional play cannot be taught through the medium of a book. To grasp it properly you must practice with your team-mates, learn the moves and learn to make sure that you are in the right position at the right time whenever you attack (that is, whenever your side has the ball), and - just as important - in the right place at the right time whenever the opposing side attacks. And always remember that one man out of position can mean a try lost.

The art of taking a rugby ball at full speed is an art that only constant practice can perfect, so you need that constant practice. Spreading your fingers and keeping your body behind the ball will help you to keep hold of the ball. It is no good saying when you have dropped a pass that it was a bad pass. Not all passes can be good ones, so when you are sent a bad one you must strive all you know to turn bad into good.

And when you are passing you must make certain that you release the ball at the right moment - and there is only one right moment - and that it goes into the arms of a colleague. You must have a good grip on the ball so that you will not send it spinning through the air and you must have perfect co-ordination of all your muscles so that you are on the right foot and perfectly poised to release the ball when the time comes. And never, never, never just fling the ball out just because you are being tackled. Make your opponents fight for the ball. Don't give it to them.

Now for kicking. Probably place-kicking - that is, kicking

at goal - gives the most trouble to youngsters. But there is also a lot of skill in the normal kick for touch, or the quick kick through for the burst. But for goodness' sake don't overdo the kick. Remember that if you are going to kick for touch, kick for touch. Don't just kick the ball in the general direction so that the opposing full-back has an easy pick-up. Try to change the direction of the attack so that the opposing defenders are caught on the wrong foot or out of position.

The quick kick through must be used when you see an opening which cannot be made by the normal passing movement or by side-stepping a man. For instance, if you see a gap ahead and you think that you can follow up your kick and catch the ball before it drops, thereby putting yourself clear of the defence, by all means kick - but then move. You must be able to complete the movement without losing your stride.

The same applies to the crossfield kick to your winger. You must kick the ball into the open space so that the wingman will be able to gather the ball and be away. And your wingman must know, of course, when the kick is coming. How he knows depends entirely on the tactics that you employ in your team.

But for goodness' sake don't kick for the sake of kicking. You must never surrender possession of the ball so easily.

Perhaps the most important kick is the place kick at goal, and you will usually find that the team which takes advantage of its kicks at goal will be the team that wins more matches than it loses.

If you are a goal kicker you will develop your own style, and it is essential that you keep to that style while remembering certain basic principles of goal-kicking. Generally speaking, the kick at goal can be divided into four separate operations - the placing of the ball, the run-up, the kick and the follow through.

Rugby Renegade

Placing the ball is a matter of personal preference. Some players like the ball to be pointing towards them, while others prefer the ball pointing towards the goal. You will have to try both systems under all conditions and see which suits you best. There can be no hard and fast rule, and you may find that you will want to use both positions under different circumstances.

The run-up is just as important as the run-up of a bowler at cricket. You will all have seen a bowler struggling when he is having trouble with his run-up to the wicket. He gets out of stride and has to concentrate so much on running that he has nothing left for the act of bowling, with the result that he sends down more bad balls than good ones.

The same will happen to any place kicker who does not have his run-up to the ball absolutely perfect. It is impossible to say how many strides you should take in your run-up because the length of run varies with each player. However, no matter how many strides you take you should practice hard and often to make certain that your rhythm is so perfect that your non-kicking foot is in the right position at the end of the run. If it isn't, or if you have to shuffle your feet near the end of the run, you will never be able to kick properly.

Most kickers run to the ball in a straight line. In other words, at the start of the run the kicker, the ball and the aiming point between the goalposts are in one straight line. This is by far the most popular run, but there are very good goal kickers, such as Billy Horne, who like to run in a curve. If that suits you, by all means run in a curve. But remember that if you run in a curve you will have to kick the ball with your instep.

Throughout the run-up to the ball and during the whole action of kicking, you must have your eye firmly on the ball. The ball must be the focal point of all your concentration, otherwise, just as is in golf, you will mishit it, with the fatal results of a slice or a pull.

Golf is very much like goal-kicking, for as well as keeping your eye on the ball you must also have perfect balance during the run-up and the actual kick. Most kickers spread their arms slightly to attain this balance. Then - again as in golf - the follow through after striking the ball is immensely important. The kicking foot should follow through in the same direction as the ball is meant to go. This might sound elementary, but you often see lads kicking for goal with an action that stops the kicking leg immediately the ball has been struck. Others swing their legs in a curve at the ball and finishing up - assuming they are right-foot kickers - with their right leg swinging away to the left. This means they have hooked at the ball, which will inevitably go off to the left.

So remember - balance, eye on the ball at all times, a perfect run-up and follow through with your kicking leg in the direction you want the ball to go.

At times, of course, goal kickers have to face the trickery of the weather conditions, and the worst menace to goal kickers is the wind. Only practice and experience will teach a goal kicker how to allow for the wind, so never lose an opportunity of practising in all conditions of wind. You will find it pays rich dividends.

In fact rugby, like all other games, demands constant practice. You just cannot get to the top without it.

Rugby Renegade

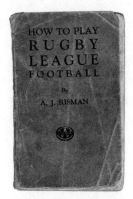

First published 1938

HOW TO PLAY
RUGBY
LEAGUE
FOOTBALL

By
A. J. RISMAN
ENGLAND AND SALFORD

Illustrated with Line Diagrams
and Action Photographs

How to Play Rugby League Football

HOW TO PLAY
RUGBY LEAGUE FOOTBALL

How the Game Began

It is a far cry from the twenty-a-side of the first international Rugby Football game ever played - that between England and Scotland on March 27th, 1871 - and the thirteen-a-side of the modern Rugby League game.

Yet the latter is a direct descendant of the former, and although this book is written in the hope that it will be of some assistance to those young players who are just taking up the Rugby League game, or who are already members of junior intermediate teams and have a genuine desire to learn, I feel that a few notes on the earlier history of Rugby and the way in which the modern Rugby League game has developed may be of interest.

Some form of Association football existed long before the handling code came into being, and it is generally understood that the idea of running with the ball in the hands originated at Rugby School in 1823. Far from being a preconceived idea, carefully thought out by any group of players, it seems to have been the sudden inspiration of a schoolboy, as the tablet to be seen at Rugby School indicates. The words inscribed on the tablet are as follows:

"William Webb Ellis picked up the ball, and for the first time, disregarding the existing rule, rushed forwards with the ball in his hands towards the opposite goal."

179

How to Play Rugby League Football

Whether Ellis had any ideas as to what his action was going to lead to is problematical. Most likely it was just sheer exuberance in the heat of the game that caused his breach of rule. Anyhow, the idea gradually caught on, and a few other Public Schools began to play Rugby. The early handlers came in for a great deal of rough treatment from the opposition, for the player with the ball seems to have been more hacked with the feet than tackled as we know it today.

Yet the game continued to grow, slowly it is true, but once Old Boys' teams began to form it was natural that other clubs should follow. But it was about thirty-seven or eight years before the first clubs came into being. The first three were Blackheath, Harlequins and Richmond, all of them still outstanding in the Rugby world today.

In those early days there were no standardised rules, although all these early teams seemed to have the common idea that hacking was an undesirable element.

Eventually it became necessary for some sort of official control, and the Rugby Union was formed in 1871. That year saw the first international - although the Scottish Rugby Union was not formed until the following year - and also the first match between Oxford and Cambridge Universities.

As I have said, there were twenty players on each side in that International, although before that time it had been no uncommon thing for there to be thirty or forty or more on each side.

From Scotland in 1877 came the suggestion to limit the number of players in a team to fifteen, and that number has remained under the Rugby Union rules ever since.

Methods of scoring varied considerably in those early days, and it was not until 1875 that a match could be won without a goal being scored, or with goals equal. In that year the number of tries was officially allowed to count. Nine years later the point system of scoring was introduced, three tries equalling a goal.

Eight years later, in 1894, occurred an incident that was destined to become history. My present club, Salford, was suspended by the Rugby Union for eight weeks for professionalism. The Union refused to recognise "broken time" payment to players, and still do not do so, and the suspension of Salford had its sequel when, in the following year - on August 29th, 1895, to be precise - a meeting at Huddersfield resulted in twenty-two clubs resigning from the Rugby Union and forming the Northern Union, all playing in one tournament; they were: Batley, Bradford, Brighouse Rangers, Broughton Rangers, Halifax, Huddersfield, Hunslet, Hull, Leeds, Leigh, Liversedge, Manningham, Oldham, Rochdale Hornet, Runcorn, St. Helens, Stockport, Tyldesley, Wakefield Trinity, Warrington, Widnes and Wigan. Curiously enough Salford, whose suspension had led to the "break", was not among the founders of the new Union, but they soon joined, together with numerous other "deserters". Membership of the Northern Union had become so big by the start of its second season that Lancashire and Yorkshire had to have separate competitions.

Next came the Northern League in 1901, with fourteen clubs competing. Eighteen clubs competed in 1902 when two divisions were formed, but in 1905 the League was reorganised into one division with no limit to the number of clubs competing.

By this time the Northern Union had made changes in the playing rules which, at foundation, it had adopted from the Rugby Union. The line-out was substituted in 1897 by a punt-out from touch, but this was itself abolished in 1902 and the 10 yards' scrummage instituted instead. Another change, designed to speed up the game, and improve it as a spectacle by avoiding deliberate waste of time, was the prohibition of touch-finding by direct kicking into touch. Then, in 1906, came the important reduction in the number of players from fifteen to thirteen.

Early payments to players were very small, and were only for"broken-time"; more in the nature of expenses and compensation for wages lost through being away from work. In 1898 full professionalism came into being, although it was stipulated that players must have an occupation in addition to that of playing Rugby. Then came the deletion of this "work clause" as it was known, and the payment of players per match played.

Further big changes took place in 1922 when kicking a goal from a mark was abolished, and the title was changed from Northern Union to the Rugby League.

It is a curiosity that the Rugby League type of game, while it has spread abroad to Australia and New Zealand, should, at home, be confined to the North of England. Efforts to establish it in the South, especially in the London area, have so far been unsuccessful, yet it is gaining in popularity in France.

So much for a very brief outline of how the Rugby League came into being. Now for a few, I hope, helpful notes on how to play it.

The Field and Its Markings

Firstly a word or two about the field-of-play. The laws of the game stipulate that it shall not exceed 110 yards in length and 75 yards in breadth, and shall be as near those dimensions as possible. Note that no minimum measurements are given, although the standard by-laws of the junior league require a space of not less than 90 yards by

60 yards, and those of the intermediate league (for players under 21 years of age on September 1st of any one season) state that clubs must provide a ground with a clear playing space of not less than 80 yards by 50 yards. The lines marking the sides of the pitch are the touch-lines, and those across the ends are the goal lines. The goal-posts, in the centre of the goal-lines, must have uprights of over 11 feet high, placed 18 feet 6 inches apart. The cross-bar should be 10 feet from the ground.

Very briefly the object of the game may be summed up as trying to score goals by kicking the ball over the cross-bar, or scoring tries by touching-down the ball behind your opponents' goal-line.

The ball, as you know, is oval in shape, and the laws of the game state it must as nearly as possible be 11 to $11^{1/2}$ inches long, 30 to 31 inches around its longest part, and 24 to $24^{1/2}$ inches around its greatest width. The weight should be from $14^{1/2}$ to $15^{1/2}$ ounces.

Naturally it would not be much of a game if the players of both sides were allowed to run hither and thither at will, chasing the ball with no restrictions on the things they could do. So there are additional markings on the field. Firstly, there is a line from 6 to 8 yards behind each goal-line, and parallel to it, called the dead-ball line, and whenever the ball, or a player holding the ball, crosses this line, the ball is dead and out of play, and the game is restarted by a drop-kick from within the centre of a line marked across the field 25 yards from the goal-line by one of the defending side. The ways of kicking a ball, drop-kick, place-kick and punt, will be described later.

The half-way line is marked across the middle of the field, and it is from the centre of the field that the kick-off takes place by means of a place-kick at the start of the game, after a goal has been scored and after half-time.

How to Play Rugby League Football

The other markings are to indicate a distance of 10 yards from either side of the half-way line, 10 yards inside the field-of-play from the touch-lines, and 5 yards inside the field-of-play from the goal-lines. The purposes of these lines need not concern you for the moment but will be made clear later in the book.

Equipment

The matter of equipment, a very important one, receives only one brief mention in the laws of the game. This is in regard to boots or shoes, without which no one is allowed to play. The law states: "No one wearing projecting nails or iron plates on any part of the boots or shoes shall be allowed to play in any match."

The reason for this should be obvious to all, for such attachments would be most dangerous and might inflict a very serious injury on another player.

This, too, should make you take great care in your choice of boots or shoes and your subsequent treatment of them. It is essential that your footwear should be comfortable, yet strong enough to withstand hard wear and tear, often in wet weather.

At the same time you must avoid heaviness and clumsiness which will only retard mobility. Get a good quality leather with soles of sufficient thickness to take a stud of anything up to three-quarters of an inch. Studs, of course, should be of leather, although if you prefer bars of leather it is quite permissible to have them.

Regular inspection of studs is imperative, for they have an annoying habit of working loose, and should you shed a stud and retain one or more of the nails you are breaking the law. Also worn studs offer but a precarious foothold, and it would be unfair to your side were you to slip up at a vital moment during a match through being improperly shod.

After a game always see that your boots are properly cleaned and dried to avoid them becoming stiff and uncomfortable. It is a good idea to give them a regular dressing with one or other of the several good leather preservatives now on the market.

Some players find it a good idea to have two pairs of boots, one pair for dry weather and one for wet.

When grounds are hard, you could wear a pair with fairly short studs, while on muddy and slippery surfaces you could favour the pair having slightly longer studs, so that you are sure of a firm foothold.

This is not essential, but if you do have only one pair of boots, you cannot take too much trouble over their condition, if you want them to last as long as possible. New boots need breaking in before they are really comfortable.

Although no stipulation about dress is made in the laws, it is the invariable custom for players to wear shorts and either a shirt or a jersey.

Your shorts should have elastic inserted round the waist, or should be so cut that they fit tight enough to "stay put" without any additional fastenings. If the elastic should by any chance break, and you require a temporary measure in order to finish a match, use string or a spare lace.

Which reminds me that boot laces need to be inspected before every game. If you adopt the general custom of winding the laces round under the insteps as well as round the top of the boots to secure additional ankle support - a very sound idea - you will find the laces have a tendency eventually to fray where they press against the sides of the soles as well as where they rub against the eyelet holes. To avoid unnecessary stoppages for the repair of broken laces, replace as soon as there is any sign of wear, and always keep a spare pair handy, and don't leave them at home when you travel to an away game!

How to Play Rugby League Football

Kicking and Fielding

As already mentioned, there are three kinds of kicks in Rugby Football. These are officially described in the laws of the game as follows:-

A Drop-kick is made by a player letting the ball fall from his hands, and kicking it as it rebounds from the ground.

A Place-kick is made by a player kicking the ball after it has been placed on the ground for the purpose.

A Punt is made by a player letting the ball fall from his hands and kicking it before it touches the ground.

The secret of good kicking of any kind is correct timing. For drop-kicks the ball should be held around the middle with a pointed end towards the ground and with the fingers spread out, and the arms at almost full stretch.

If you are moving forward the ball should be dropped as the left foot comes to the ground (for a right-footed drop-kick), the right leg swinging sharply forward and straightening out at the knee so that the foot meets the ball just after it has bounced, on the half-volley as it were.

A punt would be made similarly, except that the ball is released from the hands a little later so that the foot meets it just before it reaches the ground.

The kicking foot should follow well through and upwards in the direction of the kick and the toes should be pointed upwards. Care must be taken not to drop the ball too close to the body, else the kicking leg will not have room in which properly to straighten out and the kick will lack power.

Place-kicking has come to be regarded as something of a specialist's job, and you usually find that every team has one, sometimes two players, who stand out above their fellows in this respect. Certainly place-kicking is of great importance, for on its success depends whether or not a try is followed by a goal.

Unless the ball is correctly placed the kick will not be very successful. A small heel mark is made so that the ball can be placed with one end pointing upwards along the line of the intended kick. The ball can be either lying down or straight upright, with the lace always directly away from the kicker.

You often see the mistake made of the kicker taking a strong run up to the ball before kicking, but this tends merely to increase the margin of error in timing and direction, and does not necessarily add power.

Go back just a sufficient number of paces to give you a "running" kick whereby you get some momentum behind the ball, but let the main power come from the leg action. "Follow through" is the essential point of place-kicking.

After a try the ball can be brought back into the field-of-play, in a line with where the try was scored, as far as the kicker deems necessary. This requires practice in judging the strength of your kick in relation to wind, which may be against you, behind you or blowing across. Sometimes, therefore, you aim to kick a little lower than at other times to allow for the wind lifting the ball and to get distance, while the effect of a cross-wind must be counteracted by aiming to the right or left of the goal as the case may be.

Most place-kickers always use the same foot, but, for drop kicks or punts, it is very advisable to practice kicking with either foot.

Do not think that it is only the full-back who needs to know how to field a ball. It is true that he will have to do a great deal more of this than any other player, but occasions arise when any player in whatever position he normally plays may be called upon to catch a punt or drop-kick.

Watch the ball ceaselessly, try to judge its flight, having

regard to the strength and direction of the wind, and try to get under it so that you can form a cradle with your arms and chest. The elbows should be in to the body, and the fingers spread open. As the ball drops into the cradle the body gives slightly, and the arms and hands close round it to prevent any rebound from the chest.

Always try to avoid having to use the hands only to make a catch, for the chances are that the ball will slip through your fingers, especially if it is wet and muddy.

Running, Passing and Tackling

Before you think about giving and taking passes, you must have some idea of how to run best with the ball.

You have two choices, firstly holding the ball with two hands, all ready to pass to right or left, and, secondly, going for the line with the ball tucked under an arm.

The first method is general when you do not expect to make much ground and when you know you have a colleague, or colleagues, up in support and ready for a pass. The ball should be held about upright between the hands, with the fingers spread, and with the arms a little out in front of the body. As you move forward the hands naturally move from side to side so that an opponent cannot readily anticipate to which side you might pass.

But if you do not intend to pass, but hope to "barge through" or see a chance of going clear away for a try, the ball should be tucked under the armpit with the hands underneath, again with spread fingers. Keep it on that side of the body which is away from any would-be tackler; this will generally be the side nearer the touch-line, and then go hard and straight for your objective.

Now for passing. Practice at this can never be overdone, for a badly made pass makes it so much more difficult for your colleague, and may rob him of a scoring chance, while a badly taken pass may similarly nullify a brilliant piece of work by the man who made the pass.

The chief motive power for a pass comes from a sharp turn of the body, not from the arms as may be supposed.

Firstly, a word about direction. The pass should be made so that the ball reaches its man about waist high. As he will be moving forward with you, you must aim a little in front of him - how much will depend upon how far away he is.

Now the rules do not allow a man to be in front of the player with the ball, so that you will have to pass slightly backwards. This means that the body has to make a very definite turn. You should make a pass to the left when the left foot comes to the ground. As the right foot swings forward the body is turned sharply to the left, thus causing the arms to swing that way, and guide the ball in the required direction. Some power, it is true, comes from the arms, but it is merely supplementary to the body swing. If you start the pass with a sharp twist of the head, the body and arms will automatically follow, while this head turning will be found a help in acquiring correct direction. Never make the mistake of looking at your would-be tackler while in the act of passing the ball.

Similarly, when taking a pass, the body should be turned towards the ball. The arms should be held out in front of you, but with the elbows in towards the body, making the catching cradle, while the fingers must be apart. The palms of the hands should be slightly upwards and ready to close quickly round the ball.

If the pass has been correctly made the ball will come to you end-on, so that, should you fail to grasp it properly, it will hit your chest or arm with a good chance of you catching it as it rebounds.

Running and passing, of course, are practiced together.

How to Play Rugby League Football

You must try to become equally efficient at giving and receiving a pass on both the right and left sides, and remember, always try to work up to maximum running speed.

As for the right moment to make a pass, this depends on such things as your position in relation to your colleagues and to your opponents.

Normally, when you get the ball you should endeavour to draw the opposition towards you, and away from your colleagues before making your pass. But that should not be delayed so long that you have to try and make the pass when in the middle of being tackled.

Which brings me to the right and wrong way of making a tackle. A tackle, by the way, is described in the laws as follows:-

> "A tackle is when the holder of the ball is held
> by one or more players of the opposite side, or
> when the holder and the ball come into contact
> with the ground whilst being held."

An opponent gets away with the ball. You come across field to intercept him. As soon as you are near enough go hard at him, and throw yourself forward so as to grasp him as low as possible, round the knees or lower, in order to bring him sharply to the ground.

If your opponent is running fast and you do not go low he may avoid you by handing you off, that is, pushing you off with his hand. But by going low you are almost certain to upset his balance even if you do not manage to grasp him properly, while it will be difficult for him to hand you off.

In some games one sees rather too much bad tackling, with players being content merely to stop the progress of the opponent in possession of the ball, without any real attempt being made to bring him to the ground.

Of course, if that is the only way of stopping the opponent, use it, but remember that most referees prefer to see a proper tackle, with man and ball brought down.

Rugby League football has cut out the loose scrum that usually happens in a similar situation under Rugby Union rules. The League procedure can perhaps best be made clear by quoting the note to the law describing a tackle. It reads as follows:-

"When a player is tackled, the ball can only be brought into play with the foot, the player dropping it on the ground directly in front of him for that purpose, when it can be kicked by either side in any direction. Neither player playing the ball is allowed to stand with one foot lifted awaiting the dropping of the ball on the ground. Both players must face the respective goal-lines. If the player is on the ground he should be allowed to regain his feet, without delay, with the ball in his possession. Only one player from each side will be permitted to play the ball, and one player from each side (to act as half-back) be allowed to stand not less than 1 yard behind the players playing the ball. All other players within a radius of 10 yards must stand at least 3 yards behind the player acting as half-back. On any breach of this law the non-offending side shall be awarded a penalty kick.

"It is not imperative for the tackled player to stand erect before dropping the ball.

"A player knocked to the ground is not tackled, even if the ball touches the ground, if the tackler relinquishes his hold before the player reaches the ground."

How to Play Rugby League Football

This is called "Play the ball". But before we leave tackling there are one or two points I want to mention. Firstly, when tackling a running man from the side, always try to get your head and shoulders behind him so that he falls away from you. When tackling from the front or back try to make him fall away from the side on which you have got your head, and remember always that a man is not tackled if you release your hold before he reaches the ground. A tackle must never be half-hearted, and the risk of being hurt is not nearly as big as you may suppose. In fact, it is the hesitant sort of tackle that more often leads to mishap, than the one made with spirit and determination.

Forward Play

Now we come to the various positions on the field and some of the special duties attached to them.

In the very early days of the game there was probably no very clear idea of positional play as we know it today, and even now there is nothing in the laws of the game to say that a side shall consist of so many forwards, half-backs, three-quarters or full-backs. The only stipulation is that the game should be played by 13 players on each side, although no substitute is allowed to take the place of any player compelled to leave the field through injury or any other causes.

As the science of the game has been developed a generally accepted formation has been evolved, comprising six forwards, two half-backs, four three-quarters and a full-back.

It is in the forward formation that you get the difference in number between Rugby League and Rugby Union football, the latter generally playing eight forwards,

The player with the ball is about to drop it for a punt.
Note fingers and thumb spread out around ball

Note how player with the ball is making his pass just before an opponent gets up to tackle him or intercept the pass

although experiments have been made with seven forwards packing for the scrums.

As I have said, the Rugby League rules have eliminated the loose scrum, and it can no longer be said that a forward's main asset is strength for scrum work.

In fact, nowadays, a forward should possess speed and the ability to give and take passes equal almost to that of the three-quarters. Forwards must always try to be up with the ball, ready either to carry it forward with a dribble, or initiate a passing movement, or, on occasion, seize an opening and go over for a try.

Rules to which forwards should pay special attention are those dealing with off-side and on-side. A player is placed off-side if the ball has been kicked, touched, or is being run with by one of his own side behind him.

You cannot, however, be off-side in your own in-goal, except when one of your own side is taking a free-kick behind your own goal-line. Then all the team must be behind the ball when kicked.

An off-side player is not allowed to play the ball, actively or passively obstruct an opponent waiting for the ball. Any deliberate breach of this rule means a penalty kick to the opposition on the spot where the breach occurred, or a scrum at the spot where the ball was last played by the offending side.

Of course, they would have a penalty kick if the spot was within reasonable distance of your goal and there was a chance of the kick succeeding. But suppose your full-back has punted up-field from near his own goal-line and you, a forward, well over the half-way line, and of necessity in an off-side position, commit a breach of the rule. Then it would be better for the opposition to have a scrum near your goal-line, from which they might gain possession of the ball and score a try. Not only are you giving the opposition a chance to score, but you may also be robbing your own side of a likely score by stopping the game just when a colleague gets clean away with the ball.

Mental alertness and quick thinking will save you from breaking the rule, and the same applies in regard to knowing instantly when you have been placed on-side and can again take part in the game.

Rule 10 states:-

"An off-side player, provided he is not within the 5 yards' limit, or engaged in a 'play the ball' is placed on-side:

"(a) When an opponent has run 5 yards with the ball.

"(b) When the ball has been kicked or played by an opponent.

"(c) When one of his side has run in front of him with the ball.

"(d) When one of his side has run in front of him, having kicked the ball when behind him."

You cannot under any circumstances be placed on-side when within the 5 yards' limit, that is, when within 5 yards of your opponents' goal-line.

With regard to being put on-side by a colleague kicking the ball, remember that although he may follow-up in touch he must be in the field-of-play again before he can put you on-side. Also, remember that only the kicker can place you on-side again.

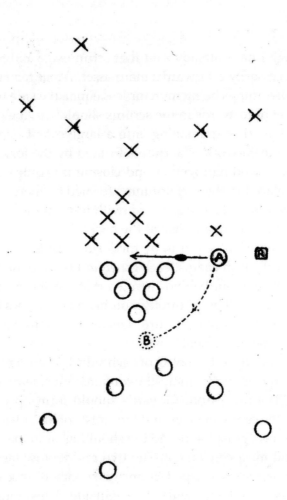

POSITIONS FOR A SCRUM
A general formation for a scrum in mid-field. The attacking
side, indicated by circles, has the Loose Head on the Referee's
side. As soon as the Scrum-Half (A) has put the ball in the
scrum, he retires to position B. The Referee's position is
shown by the letter R.

How to Play Rugby League Football

Scrums

Although I have already said that scrummage ability is not now necessarily a forward's main asset, it still remains true that, other things being more or less equal, the side with the better set of forwards in the scrums should win the game.

And good scrummaging is to a large extent dependent on good team-work. A scrum is formed by the forwards of each team binding together and closing up so that the ball can be placed in the sort of tunnel formed by their legs. The six forwards pack, as it is called, with three in the front row, two in the second, and one at the back.

When the ball is put in by the scrum-half the two packs of forwards push against each other and try to hook the ball with their feet out behind them so that the scrum-half can gather it and either go through on his own, or pass back to the stand-off half who, in turn, sets the three-quarters going on a passing movement.

That, briefly, is the object of each side. But strong shoving alone is not enough. Firstly, the forwards must learn to pack tightly. The three front forwards should form up with the arms of the centre man around the waists of his outside men, they, in turn, grasping round the shoulders or in the manner they find most convenient. The two middle row men, with their inner arms clasped round each other's body, pack down behind them with their outside arms round the outside men of the front row. They should get their shoulders well behind the front row men and have their heads tucked well down. The rear forward packs down similarly behind the two middle men. The legs should be slightly bent at the knees so that a good shove can be given, but get your legs back far enough for the shove to be forward and not upward.

There are certain things that must be observed when a scrum is formed. Firstly, the front row forwards on each side must be in a straight line so that the tunnel between the legs of the two lines is clearly defined. Also, the middle forward must not have an arm loose.

All the forwards must keep their feet on the ground until the ball has been put into the tunnel, and at no time may any forward have both feet off the ground at the same time. The two front row forwards, on the further side from where the ball is put in , may put their legs across the tunnel to prevent the ball from going straight through, but, obviously, they will put across only one leg each.

When the two front lines pack against each other, one man of each row, of course, will have his head on the outside of the two lines. This is termed the loose head, and it is compulsory for the attacking side to have the loose head on the side of the scrum on which the referee stands.

When the ball has been put in, it can only be heeled out from behind the front row forwards. It is usual for one man, the middle forward of the front row, to be a specialised hooker. That is, he is specially adept at hooking the ball with his foot as it comes in, and of heeling it backwards. The middle forward is only allowed to strike with the foot furthest from where the ball is put in, so it is necessary that he should be equally facile with both feet.

A successful heel brings us to the duties of the half-backs, but before passing to that subject there is more to be said about scrums.

Occasions may arise when the captain may decide that instead of the ball being heeled straight back, the pack shall wheel either to the right or left - screwing the pack is the term used in the laws of the game - and take the ball with them.

It is the duty of the scrum leader to decide which way the

wheel is to be made, and all the forwards must appreciate at once what is intended, so that they can act together.

The front row men shove in the opposite direction to the intended wheel - to the left for a right wheel, and to the right for a left wheel. Assuming it is a right wheel, as the pack is screwed round, the ball, naturally, will come towards the right of the second row. The man there then breaks away from the scrum and endeavours to take the ball with him on the side of the scrum further from the opposing forwards. The other second row forward and the rear forward also break loose to back him up.

This move, if smartly executed, and having about it an element of the unexpected, can lead to a most successful concerted dribble, whereby much ground can be made.

Alternatively, it may provide an opportunity for one of the forwards to pick up the ball and start a passing movement before the pack can break up, and the opposing forwards concentrate on helping in defence.

Dribbling, by the way, should be constantly practiced, for a Rugby ball, by reason of its shape, is not easy to control. Keep the ball close to the feet, watch the ball closely, and don't try to go too fast. Use the knee to keep the ball down and propel it more rather with the shins or the side of the foot than with the toes.

The duties of forwards after a scrum has broken up are best left until we come to tactics in a later chapter, so now to the work of the half-backs.

Half-back Play

Successful half-back play depends much on the understanding that can be developed between the scrum-half and the stand-off half.

These two players are the connecting link between the

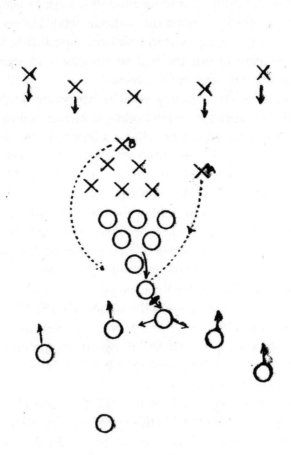

POSITIONS AFTER A PACK HAS HEELED
The ball has been heeled by the attackers, who are indicated
by circles. The defending Scrum-Half (A) moves forward to
try to tackle the attacking Scrum-Half who has the ball, and
the defending Loose Forward (B) comes round on the blind
side to prevent a break-through there.

forwards and the three-quarters, and on their ability depends much of the success of the more spectacular side of the game - good passing movements.

One of the duties of the scrum-half is to put the ball into the scrum, which he must do without delay. He can either roll the ball in, or throw it in in a downward direction. He must take care to put the ball in straight, and must then immediately retire behind the pack.

He must watch carefully what is happening to the ball, and if his forwards succeed in heeling it, he must immediately pounce upon it. Usually, he will pass it back to the stand-off half, but he often has opportunities of going away on his own, or starting a dribble, or even punting up and across field, for the rest of the side to follow up. Sometimes, also, he may get the ball from a scrum in front of the opposing goal, and may be in a position to try a drop goal. This calls for quick thinking, so that the kick can be made without danger of the ball being smothered, while you must get in your kick before an opponent has a chance to tackle you.

With regard to the pass to the stand-off half, this must be instantaneous. No time should be wasted in picking up the ball. It should be gathered and flung out in one movement, even if it means falling full length to do it. Accuracy of direction and height is necessary.

If the opposing side heel the ball the scrum-half must dash round to try and tackle the opposing scrum-half before the latter has time to dispose of the ball or break away.

Should the opposing forwards try to start a dribble or forward rush it is the job of the scrum-half to try and stop them. Either he must dash in and hold the man in possession, or if it is a dribble he must seize his chance to fall on the ball or, if possible, pick it up and try to pass it.

On the stand-off depends very largely the kind of attack that is to be initiated.

If he gets the ball cleanly and quickly from his scrum-half he will have time to draw the opponent marking him, usually the opposite stand-off half, and then set his three-quarters going by passing to one of his centres, either to left-centre or right-centre, according to which side he thinks has the better chance of getting away.

Instead of a pass, he may use a short punt across field for a wing three-quarter to follow-up, but in this case he should try to judge the strength and direction of his kick so that his own colleague has a chance of racing the opposing wing man for the ball.

Another method of attack is for the stand-off half to go forward on his own and then, when his forwards break from the pack and follow him up, to pass to one of them instead of to his three-quarters.

Always he must strive, in conjunction with his scrum-half, to maintain an element of surprise about the attacks, keeping the opposition guessing as to what is going to happen next.

I have already told you how the ball is brought into play again after a tackle, by a play-the-ball. Here, you may remember, one player of each side endeavours to play the ball with the foot as the tackled man puts it on the ground. One player on each side acts as a half-back, and each man playing the ball will, of course, endeavour to hook it back to his half-back.

It is usual for one of the forwards to take up this impromptu role of half-back, for this leaves a maximum number of backs ready for any open movement, thus not robbing the attack of any efficiency and penetrating power. Forwards, therefore, should study half-back play.

How to Play Rugby League Football

Three-quarter Play

Ability to give and take passes accurately and cleanly, and speed in running with the ball, are special attributes of the three-quarter. Theirs is the real job of attack. Nothing finer in the game is to be seen than the ball going along the whole line, and perhaps back again, with ground being made all the time, until one of them gets away for a dash over the line for a try.

The three-quarters should never be in a line square across the field. If play is in mid-field the two centre men will be in advance of the wing men so that the latter can take a backward pass.

If play is over to one side of the field, such as a 10 yard scrum after the ball has gone into touch, the three-quarters should be in a line diagonally across field, each a few yards further back than the other.

When play is in mid-field and one of the centres gets the ball, he has a choice of things he can do. He may pass to his own outside, but if that man is marked or likely to be tackled as soon as he gets the ball, he can transfer to his fellow centre, and so to the opposite wing man.

Another alternative is for him to punt ahead of one of the outsides, or, if the defence should leave a gap, to try and go through himself.

Always, however, a three-quarter should try to make some ground with the ball and try to draw the defence before passing. At the same time he must not hang on too long, and much of the art of three-quarter play comes from that nicety of judgement in timing the pass or the kick. Nothing is to be gained, usually, from getting rid of the ball as soon as you receive it, so be always alert to the situation and the disposition of the defenders. When in possession of

A good tackle. Note how the man making the tackle has gone low with his head behind the man with the ball.

A Scrum-Half passing out from a scrum. Note how pass is being made as a continuous movement with the gathering of the ball.

the ball try to draw one or more opponents away from a colleague and then pass to him so that he can go through the gap in defence.

Centre three-quarters, especially, should acquire the habit of running straight in order to avoid cramping their wing men and, perhaps, forcing them into touch.

As soon as you have passed the ball back, support your colleague by dropping into line just behind and to the side of him. The reason for this is that if you have passed to a wing man you must be ready, in an on-side position, to take a return pass, while if you, as a centre, have passed to your other centre he may find it impracticable to pass out to his wing or to kick to either side, and may want to return the ball to you after the man, or men, marking you have had their attention drawn from you.

Always be ready for the unexpected, for surprise is the essence of attack. Sometimes, for instance, a three-quarter may feint to pass to a colleague, drawing the defence towards that man, and then use a short punt over the opponent coming up to tackle him, and use his speed to race that man for the ball. Remember that your opponent has to turn before he can chase the ball while you can go straight ahead.

When the opposition are in possession, however, the three-quarters have much to do in defence. Each must mark his opposite number carefully, must be ready to tackle, to intercept a pass, and generally lend a hand in stopping forward rushes. At the same time they must all be ever ready to seize a chance of turning defence into attack. This entails watching not only the opposition but also having a general idea of where your colleagues are placed, for a wild pass is worse than useless. In fact it may give an opponent just the chance he wanted of breaking through or trying a drop at goal.

How to Play Rugby League Football

Full-back Play

Full-back play calls for certain definite qualifications and of these the most important, perhaps, is ability in fielding and kicking. He must be a sure and safe catcher of the ball and must develop a fine judgement of the ball's flight and the effect upon it of wind. He must realise that a wind blowing in the opposite direction to the flight of the ball tends to give it a higher trajectory so that it will drop short, while a cross or angular wind will tend to give the ball a curved flight. The judgement will only come with careful practice, and until is is acquired a full-back will not gain a reputation as having a "safe pair of hands".

It is the full-back's job to watch for the long punt up field over the heads of his own three-quarters and to run into position for a catch.

Hesitancy in starting forward may result in your arriving just too late to position yourself for a good catch and you may be forced to try and catch the ball with your hands alone without the help of the cradled arms and body. This is usually a sign of slow judgement, though there may be rare occasions when a full-back cannot possibly get there in time for a catch. He should avoid letting the ball bounce, if at all possible, but when he has to do so he must be ready to move instantly in any direction. A Rugby ball, because of its shape, bounces at all sorts of unexpected angles and the full-back must watch and pounce just as quickly as possible.

It is the full-back who will be most interested in what is termed a mark. This is when the ball is caught direct, and at the first attempt from a kick, knock-on, or throw-forward by an opponent, and must be claimed by the catcher making a mark with his heel at the spot where the catch was made, or by holding up one hand.

A fair catch entitles the side of the player making it to a free kick from any spot behind the mark on a line parallel to the touch-line. The ball may not be kicked into touch unless it first bounces in the field of play. All the players in the team must bear in mind, when making a punt, the possibility of an opponent making a fair catch and watch the direction of their kick accordingly.

A big advantage of the fair catch to a full-back is that it prevents him being tackled by an opponent who may have followed up the kick and have got near enough to the back to tackle him had he not claimed the catch. This also emphasises the importance of good catching, for if the full-back fumbles the ball- perhaps lets it slip through his hands or catches the ball on the bounce - an opposing forward, following smartly up, might gain possession of the ball and get in for a try. Also a back must realise that if he is tackled with the ball, a play-the-ball takes place and the opposition have gained ground by as much, perhaps, as half the length of the field.

Another aspect of full-back play is in watching for the break-away by an opposing three-quarter, or other player, and in going across to tackle him.

The full-back should follow closely the mid-field play as it moves from side to side of the field and adjust his own position accordingly, trying to anticipate where the opposition are most likely to get away on a dash for the line. The ideal is for him to be so positioned that he can rush across to stop the opponent without having to retreat backwards at the same time. In fact, if he can go across and slightly forward at the same time he should do so.

As he is the last line of defence he must be a sure and fearless tackler and must be ever ready for such things as an attempt to hand-off, feint, swerve or side-step on the part of the opponent.

My advice to full-backs is to study the other positions on the field, especially the art of three-quarter play, for tries are very often caused through a full-back joining his three-quarters and making an extra man, usually taking a pass from one of the centres and bursting through.

Tactics

Tactics, dictated, of course, by the captain, depend to some extent on the general capabilities of the team as a whole, on the strengths and weaknesses of the opposing side, and, sometimes, on the weather and the conditions of the ground.

Obviously a dry ground and ball are best suited to good passing movements, while a sticky or slippery ground and a greasy ball make the holding of passes difficult and take away from the speed of the three-quarters. Then the brunt of the work will fall on the forwards.

If the opponents early prove themselves specially quick in marking and breaking up attempted passing movements a captain may instruct his own forwards to persevere with a series of concerted rushes with the ball at their feet.

This mention of tackling reminds me, by the way, that I wanted to say a few more words in this chapter about the duties of forwards.

If you think back to my remarks on scrums you will recall that the scrum-half puts the ball in, then returns behind the pack to wait for the ball when it is heeled.

As soon as one side heels, the opposing scrum-half will come round the pack on the side the ball was put in, in order to try and prevent the scrum-half of the pack heeling from getting the ball away.

At the same time the half in possession must not be allowed to get away on the blind side of the scrum (the side away from where the ball was put in), so the rear forward, called the loose forward, of the side who has not succeeded in heeling the ball breaks away from the pack and comes round ready to tackle.

When a pack finds that it is repeatedly losing the scrums because the opposition are stronger or are hooking better, all the forwards must be ready to break quickly form the scrum and help in tackling, though this applies specially to the man in the rear and the two second row men. The latter, as soon as they get their heads up, must take in the situation at a glance and move into position accordingly.

If the full-back gets the ball and sees the possible chance of a good run up field he should go, and one of the centre three-quarters should drop back to take his place. Each three-quarter, by the way, marks his opposite number, and any movement by the three-quarters should always be backed up by the forwards.

Whatever tactics may be decided upon at any stage of the game, they depend for their success on team work, so give your captain whole-hearted co-operation. Play to order, but, at the same time, be ready to act on your own initiative when need arises. And one final word. Study the laws of the game carefully.

If you find anything in the laws about which you are not quite clear, do not hesitate to ask a player of greater experience. All of us are keen to see the game of Rugby League football grow, and whatever knowledge of the game we have, we are only too willing to pass on to others. And remember, first and last, to play the game as it is intended to be played, in the right spirit, and as fairly and cleanly as possible.

PLAN OF THE FIELD

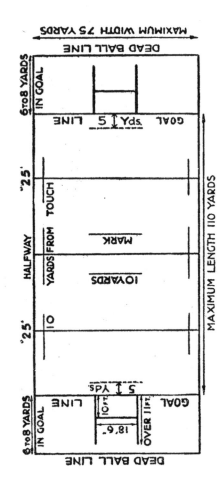

NOTE. — The field-of-play shall not exceed 110 yards in length and 75 yards in breadth, and should be as near those dimensions as practicable. The dead-ball lines should be not less than 6 yards or more than 8 yards from the goal-lines. The touch-lines and goal-lines should be suitably marked on the turf. In marking out the field-of-play, care should be taken to show clearly the half-way, 25 yards, and dead-ball lines, and to indicate the 10 yards from the half-way and touch-lines, as shown in the accompanying plan of the field. Marks should be made with whiting or chalk, not sawdust or ruts cut in the turf.

THE LAWS
OF THE
GAME OF FOOTBALL
AS PLAYED BY
THE RUGBY FOOTBALL LEAGUE

Reprinted by permission of the Rugby Football League [1938].

I. INTRODUCTION

1. The Rugby League Game of Football should be played by 13 players on each side, but when once the game is started substitutes shall not be introduced to take the place of any player compelled to leave the field of play through injury or any other cause.

Number of Players

The field of play shall not exceed 110 yards in length and 75 yards in breadth, and shall be as near those dimensions as practicable.

Field of Play

The Boundary Lines of the field-of-play shall be suitably marked, and shall be called Goal-Lines at the ends and Touch-Lines at the sides.

Boundary Lines

On each goal-line and equidistant from the touch-lines shall be two upright posts, called Goal-Posts, exceeding 11 feet in height, placed 18 feet 6 inches apart and joined by a cross-bar 10 feet from the ground. The cross-bar shall not extend beyond the goal-posts.

Goal Posts

How to Play Rugby League Football

Ball	The game shall be played with an Oval Ball of as nearly as possible the following size and weight: Length..11 to 11 $^{1/2}$ in. Length circumference................30 to 31 in. Width circumference..............24 to 24 $^{1/2}$ in. Weight ....14 $^{1/2}$ to 15 $^{1/2}$ oz.
Objects of the Game	The object of the game shall be to cross the opponents' goal-line to score Tries, and to kick a ball over the cross-bar and between the posts to score Goals.

GLOSSARY - OFFICIALS -SCORING
Glossary of Terms

2. The following terms occur in the Laws and have the respective meanings attached to each:-

Dead-Ball Lines	DEAD-BALL LINES - Not less than 6 or more than 8 yards behind and equidistant from each goal-line, and parallel thereto, shall be lines called Dead-Ball Lines, and if the ball or player holding the ball touch or cross these lines the ball shall be dead and out of play.
In-Goal	IN-GOAL - The portions of the ground immediately at the ends of the field-of-play and between the touch-lines, extended to the dead-ball lines, are called In-Goal. The goal-lines are In-Goal.

NOTE.— A ball placed on the goal-line by an attacking player is a try, and by a defending player a touch-down.

A ball kicked into the field-of-play from in-goal by a defending player, and blown back to in-goal may be touched down by a defending player.

When a ball is kicked in the air and drops into touch from in-goal a scrum must take place 5 yards from the goal-line opposite the spot from whence it was kicked.

If the ball, or a player holding the ball in his own in-goal, touches the referee, a dead ball shall be awarded at the spot, and a drop-out must be taken; in the event of a player holding the ball touching the referee, in his opponents' in-goal, a try shall be allowed at the spot, although he may not have grounded the ball.

TOUCH.— Those portions of the ground immediately at the sides of the field-of-play and between the goal-lines, if extended, are called Touch. The touch-lines are In-Touch.

Touch

NOTE.— A player may be in-touch and yet play the ball with his foot if the ball be not in-touch. A ball crossing the touch-lines in the air and caught by a player not himself in-touch is deemed to have dropped in the field-of-play. A ball crossing the touch-line in the air and knocked back into the field-of-play by a player in-touch jumping in the air and landing in the field-of-play is deemed to have dropped in the field-of-play; if the player, however, should land in-touch the ball is in-touch at the spot. A ball kicked across the touch-line by a player who running on jumps from the field-of-play and knocks it back in the field-of-play, the player landing in-touch is deemed to have dropped in the field-of-play.

If a player deliberately throws the ball in-touch, the Referee shall order a penalty kick to the opposite side if thrown forward, or a ten yards' scrum from the spot where it went in-touch, if not forward. A ball kicked over the touch-line in the air and then blown back again before touching the ground shall be considered as not in-touch.

Touch-in-Goal TOUCH-IN-GOAL.— Those portions of the ground immediately at the four corners of the field-of-play and between goal and touch-line, if respectively extended, are called Touch-in-Goal. The corner posts and flags, if any, are Touch-in-Goal.

> NOTE.— *A player may himself be in touch-in-goal and yet play the ball with his foot if it be not in touch-in-goal.*

A DROP-KICK is made by a player letting the ball fall from his hands and kicking it as it rebounds from the ground. *Drop-Kick*

A PLACE-KICK is made by a player kicking the ball after it has been placed on the ground for the purpose. *Place-Kick*

A PUNT is made by a player letting the ball fall from his hands and kicking it before it touches the ground. *Punt*

A FREE-KICK is awarded for a fair catch and may be a drop-kick, a place-kick, or a punt, but it must be in the direction of the opponents' goal-line, and across the kicker's goal-line if kicked from behind same. The ball must drop in the field-of-play. A goal cannot be scored from a free-kick. *Free-Kick*

A PENALTY-KICK is imposed by way of a penalty, and may be a drop-kick, a place-kick, or a punt, but it must be in the direction of the opponents' goal-line. The ball may be kicked into touch at the full. A goal may be scored from a penalty kick. *Penalty-Kick*

Held

HELD is when the player holding the ball cannot play it, and his progress has been effectually stopped.

Tackle

A TACKLE is when the holder of the ball is held by one or more players of the opposite side, or when the holder and the ball come into contact with the ground whilst being held.

> *NOTE.— When a player is tackled, the ball can only be brought into play with the foot, the player dropping it on the ground directly in front of him for that purpose, when it can be kicked by either side in any direction. Neither player playing the ball is allowed to stand with one foot lifted awaiting the dropping of the ball on the ground. Both players must face the respective goal-lines. If the player is on the ground he should be allowed to regain his feet, without delay, with the ball in his possession. Only one player from each side will be permitted to play the ball, and one player from each side (to act as half-back) be allowed to stand not less than 1 yard behind the players playing the ball. All other players within a radius of 10 yards behind the*

player acting as half-back. On any breach of this law the non-offending side shall be awarded a penalty-kick.

It is not imperative for the tackled player to stand erect before dropping the ball.

A player knocked to the ground is not tackled, even if the ball touches the ground, if the tackler relinquishes his hold before the player reaches the ground.

A SCRUM is formed by players of each side binding together and closing up in readiness to allow the ball to be put on the ground between them.

Scrum: How Formed

> *NOTE.— When a scrum is ordered by the Referee it must be formed so as to provide a clear opening, or tunnel, in which to insert the ball, and the close observance of the following instructions is imperative:—*

(a) The front row forwards on each side must form in a straight line so as to provide a clearly defined tunnel. The middle forward must not have one arm loose during the scrum, and can only strike with the foot farthest from where the ball is being put in.

(b) The forwards must keep their feet on the ground until the half-back has put the ball into the tunnel, and at no time must any forward have both feet off the ground at the same time.

(c) The two front row forwards on the far side of the scrum may put their legs across the tunnel so as to prevent the ball from going through.

(d) The half-back must put the ball in without delay, either by rolling, or pitching it into the centre of the scrum by a downward movement.

(e) Immediately the half-back has put the ball in he must retire behind the pack.

(f) The ball must come out from behind the front row of forwards, and on no account should it be allowed to be played if it comes out by way of the tunnel.

(g) The loose forward must not pack at the side of the scrum.

It is the duty of the Referee to order the ball to be put in until it comes out as stated, and to award a penalty kick for any

<u>infringement, providing the non-offending side has not gained an advantage.</u>

The Referee may order the ball to be put into the scrum from either side he may choose. It is compulsory for the attacking side to have the loose head on the side of the scrum on which the Referee stands.

It is permissible for a player at the rear of the scrum to detach himself and pick up the ball to bore his way through the pack, or for a player in the scrum to hold the ball with his knees, or for the players on either side in the scrum to screw the pack and take the ball with them.

A TRY is gained by the player who first *Try* puts his hand on the ball on the ground in his opponents' In-Goal, always providing that the said player is not in touch, touch-in-goal, or over the dead-ball line.

> *NOTE.— When a try has been scored, the Referee shall see that the ball is taken out correctly for the kick for goal, or he may delegate the duty to a touch-judge.*
>
> *If a player bounces or drops the ball from his hands, instead of touching it down, it is not a try. If an attacking player is checked, but not tackled by an opponent, over the goal-line, and both go to the ground together, and the ball*

is touched down by both of them at the same time, it is a try.

If an attacking player loses possession of the ball over the goal-line, the ball going in a forward direction, he shall be deemed to have knocked-on, and a dead ball be ordered. A player who crosses the opponents' goal-line with the ball in his possession, and before grounding it touches the Referee, shall be allowed a try at the spot.

Touch-Down

A TOUCH-DOWN is made by the player who first puts his hand on the ball on the ground in his own In-Goal.

NOTE.— If a defending player receives the ball in the field-of-play and runs over his own goal-line, kicks the ball, and is then obstructed by an opponent, a dead ball should be allowed.

Goal

A GOAL is obtained by kicking the ball from the field-of-play over the opponents' cross-bar, whether it touches the cross-bar or the goal-posts or not, except from a punt, a kick-off, a drop-out, or a free kick.

NOTE.— If the ball has gone over the cross-bar, and is then blown back, it is a goal.

If the ball kicked for goal touches in transit an opposing player before going over the cross-bar, it is a goal.

If the ball hits the cross-bar or goal-posts and afterwards rebounds from a defending player over the cross-bar, it is not a goal.

If a player, kicks the ball towards his opponents' goal and following up kicks the ball again and it goes over the cross-bar it is a goal.

If a ball kicked for goal falls short in front of the posts, then bounces over the cross-bar, it is not a goal.

KNOCKING-ON AND THROWING-FORWARD and propelling the ball by the hand or arm in the direction of the opponents' In-Goal.

Knocking-on and Throwing-Forward

NOTE.— The ball is not necessarily knocked-on in every case in which it goes forward off a player's hands, e.g., in the case of a ball rebounding off the hands of a player who is standing still. The Ball is not deemed to be knocked-on unless the Referee is satisfied that there has been some active forward movement of the player's hands.

A rebound is not a knock-on, and therefore no fair-catch can be made therefrom, or a penalty given.

If a ball is passed back, but after alighting on the ground is blown forward, the pass is good.

The ball is not considered to be

knocked-on when a player charges down an opponents' kick.

Fair-Catch

A FAIR-CATCH is a catch made direct, and at the first attempt, from a kick, knock-on, or throw forward, by one of the opposite side, when the catcher must claim the same by immediately making a mark with his heel at the spot where he made the catch, or by holding up his hand.

NOTE.— A Fair Catch can be made in a player's own In-goal, in which case the opposing players may line up to but not beyond the goal-line.

Play-the-Ball and Play-on

PLAY-THE-BALL and PLAY-ON are verbal instructions given by the Referee to the players to indicate his decision for play to proceed when any doubt arises regarding an infringement, or for any other cause.

Kick-off

KICK-OFF is a place-kick from the centre of the field-of-play—
(a) To start the game,
(b) After a goal, by the side against which such goal has been scored, or
(c) After half-time, by the opposite side to that which started the game.

When the ball is being kicked off all the kicker's side must be behind the ball, otherwise a scrum shall be allowed at the centre; the opposite side must not approach within ten yards of the ball, otherwise another kick-off shall be allowed. If the ball fails to reach the ten yards' line, or pitches into touch, the Referee must order a scrum at the centre.

> *NOTE.— The ten yards referred to means ten yards off the ball and parallel with the half-way line. A ball having reached the ten yards and is then blown back shall be considered as in play.*

DROP-OUT is a drop-kick from within the centre of the half-way line, after a try is scored, or from within the centre of the 25 yards' line after a dead ball, and from the centre of the goal-line after a touch-down, within which lines the opposite side may not charge or move about the lines with the intention of obstructing the kicker, otherwise another drop-out shall be allowed. In the case of a drop-out from the goal-line, the lines referred to are 5 yards from the goal-line. If the ball fails to reach the half-way line or the 25 yards' line, or pitches into touch at the full, a scrum must take place at the centre of either the half-way line, or the 25 yards' line, as the case may be. If the ball fails to reach the 5 yards' line from a touch-down, pitches in touch at the full, or rebounds dead from the goal-posts, a scrum shall be ordered in the centre 5 yards out from the goal-line.

> *NOTE.— If a player punts the*

Drop-Out

ball or goes beyond the half-way line, 25 yards' line, or goal-line to drop-out, the Referee must order a scrum at the centre of the half-way or 25 yards' line, as the case may be, and 5 yards out from the centre of the goal-line in the case of a drop-out from there.

A ball having reached the half-way, 25 or 5 yards' lines, as the case may be, and is then blown back shall be considered as in play.

II. REFEREE AND TOUCH JUDGES

REFEREE.

3. In all matches a Referee and two Touch Judges shall be appointed.

POWERS OF REFEREE

Powers of Referee

It shall be the duty of the Referee to enforce the Laws of the Game and to decide all matters of fact (except as to Touch and Touch-in-Goal play, as hereinafter provided), but as to matters of Law there shall be a right of appeal to the Council, in accordance with Law No. 23 hereinafter mentioned.

He shall keep a record of the game, and act as time-keeper, with the power to allow extra time for delays.

He shall, at his discretion, allow for

time wasted, lost through accident or other cause; suspend or terminate the game whenever by reason of darkness, interference by spectators, or other causes, he may deem it necessary; but in all cases in which a game is so terminated he shall report the same to the League, or other body under whose jurisdiction the game is played, who shall deal with the matter.

He shall, in the event of any misbehaviour on the part of any player, caution the offender, and if the offence is repeated, or in the case of violent conduct without any previous caution, he shall be empowered to order the offending player off the field-of-play, and shall within 48 hours transmit the name of such player, together with the nature of the offence, to the League, or Union, and a copy of same to the player's Club.

He shall, if he thinks fit, send a player off the field-of-play who persistently and wilfully breaks the Laws of the Game (by systematically lying off-side, repeatedly putting the ball unfairly into a scrum, wilfully wasting time, or other like offence) as such action is deemed misconduct. Before taking this extreme course, however, he should warn the offending player.

The power of the Referee extends to offences committed when play has been temporarily suspended, and when the ball is out of play.

When the Referee penalises a player he should state to such player his reason for doing so, and the player must not question the point.

When players are in doubt as to a tackle, or a Law being infringed, the Referee shall indicate his decision, either by blowing his whistle, or by giving verbal instructions to "play the ball".

The Referee shall accept all decisions of neutral Touch Judges as to Touch and Touch-in-Goal play, and he may consult in cases where the ball may have gone over the dead-ball line, but in every other respect shall have sole control of the game, and may act without awaiting any appeal.

NOTE.— In cases where circumstances in connection with a match are likely to be made the subject of official investigation, Referees and the Touch Judges are requested to decline being interviewed, or to give any information in any form pending the enquiry.

DUTIES OF TOUCH JUDGES

Duties of Touch Judges

4. It shall be the duty of Touch Judges to decide when and where the ball goes into touch, or touch-in-goal, and to report to the Referee any rough or foul play, or obstruction which may have escaped his notice. Each Touch Judge shall carry a

white flag and shall take one side of the ground, outside the field-of-play.

NOTE.— When the ball or player carrying the ball, touches or crosses the touch-line, the Touch Judge must stand with flat UPLIFTED at the point where the ball goes into touch or the player entered touch until a scrum has been formed.

When the ball drops directly into touch from a kick, and consequently has to be taken back to the place from whence it was kicked, the Touch Judge must WAVE his flag above his head until he is observed by the Referee.

When the ball or the player carrying it goes into touch-in-goal, the Touch Judge should immediately run to the spot and WAVE his flag over his head.

When a Touch Judge has gone behind the goal-posts to assist a Referee in deciding whether or not a goal has been scored, he should RAISE his flag above his head if a goal has been scored; if otherwise, he should WAVE his flag across his body, the flag pointing downwards. (The Referee must accept the decision of a neutral Touch Judge he has sent behind.)

Touch Judges should always hold themselves in readiness to assist the Referee in the detection of rough or foul play, or obstruction, and in the case of the latter to point out to the Referee, if necessary, the place where the ball dropped. Having made a report, they should return to their place outside the field-of-play, and the Referee should then decide what action should be taken.

EXAMPLES:
(a) A player, running with the ball, kicks into the field-of-play, away from touch, and follows up to regain possession, or to put his colleagues "on-side".
(b) A player passes the ball to one of his own side and follows up for the repass.

In the above or similar cases, where it is plain that the ball is not going toward touch, but clearly into the field-of-play, Touch Judges must devote their particular attention to the player who has kicked or passed the ball, and in the event of his being obstructed or interfered with in following up, the Touch Judge seeing the offence must immediately report to the Referee by advancing into the field-of-play with his flag UPLIFTED, until he attracts the attention of the Referee. He should, meanwhile, be careful not to lose sight of the offending player.

INTERFERENCE OF TOUCH JUDGES

5. In case of any undue interference or improper conduct by a Touch Judge, the Referee shall report the circumstance to the League or other body having jurisdiction over him, who shall deal with the matter.

Interference of Touch Judges

DUTIES OF REFEREE

6. The Referee must carry a whistle, the blowing of which shall stop the game; he must whistle in the following cases:—

(a) When an infringement takes place whereby the side committing it gains an advantage.

Duties of Referee

> *NOTE.— There is, unfortunately, a pronounced tendency on the part of Referees to whistle immediately a Law has been infringed without waiting to see who gains the advantage of the infringement. The Referee should not whistle when the non-offending side gains*

an advantage. The advantage rule cannot be applied to any infringement in in-goal by the attacking side, and should rarely be applied when an attacking side infringes near its opponents' goal-line. (See Law 22.)

(b) When a player makes and claims a fair-catch.

NOTE.— The Referee must award a penalty-kick if he thinks a fair-catch would have been made had not an off-side player, through his proximity and not returning beyond the 5 yards' limit, rendered such fair-catch more difficult.

(c) When he notices rough or foul play or misconduct.

NOTE.— Reckless kicking at the ball when an opponent is in the act of gathering it must be dealt with as foul play.

Wasting time is misconduct, and the offending players should be cautioned by the Referee, and if offending again should be ordered off the field-of-play.

A player sent off the field-of-play must proceed immediately to the dressing room and take no further part in the game.

(d) When he considers the continuation of play dangerous.

> *NOTE. — The game should not be stopped for trivial causes. If the players play the game in the spirit of the Laws very few cases of danger should arise. When, however, cases do arise, e.g. when a tackled player does not play the ball or is prevented from doing so by the opposition, the Referee should award a penalty-kick, instead of simply ordering a scrum on the plea of danger.*

> *If a player is hurt, the Referee should not whistle until the ball is out of play, unless such player is in a position that continuance of play would entail further danger.*

> *No person, except players and Touch Judges, should be allowed on the field-of-play during the game unless with the consent of the Referee.*

(e) When he allows a decision given by a Touch Judge.

> *Note. — Should a Touch Judge uplift his flag when the ball has alighted in touch from a mark, under the mistaken impression that the kick was from a penalty, or should he signal "ball back" when the ball has been touched in*

transit and alighted in touch, the touch in transit having escaped his notice, or in any similar case arising directly out of incidents that have happened in the field-of-play, and not in connection with touch or touch-in-goal play, the decision given by the Touch Judge should not be allowed by the Referee.

(f) When he wishes to stop the game for any purpose.

(g) If the ball, or a player running with the ball, touches him.

NOTE.— If the ball, or player carrying it, touches the Referee in the field-of-play, the Referee shall order a scrum at the spot.

If a player carrying the ball in his opponents' in-goal touches an official or spectator, a try shall be allowed at the spot where such official or spectator was touched.

If a player carrying the ball in his own in-goal touches an official or spectator, a dead ball shall be awarded at the spot, and a drop-out must be taken, unless the player has run behind his own goal-line, in which case the scrum shall take place 5 yards out.

If the ball not in the possession

of a player touches an official or
spectator in in-goal a dead ball
shall be awarded.

(h) If the ball becomes deflated.
   NOTE.— The ball is out-of-play
   immediately it becomes deflated.

(i) At half-time and no-side, but he shall
   not whistle until the ball be held, or out
   of play.
   NOTE.— At half-time the
   interval should not exceed five
   minutes, and may be dispensed
   with by mutual consent between
   teams.

   In the event of a free-kick or a
   penalty-kick being granted, a try
   obtained, or a scrum ordered, the
   kick must be allowed, or the
   scrum must take place, even
   though time has expired.

7. The Referee having given a decision   *Referee cannot*
on any point, other than touch and Touch-   *alter his*
in-Goal play, cannot under any   *decision*
circumstances alter it.
   NOTE.— When the Referee
   blows his whistle the game must
   stop, even if he has blown it
   accidentally.

III. MODE OF PLAY - DEFINITIONS.

Captains to toss

CHOICE OF IN-GOAL OR KICK-OFF.

8. The Captains of the respective sides shall toss for the choice of In-Goal or the Kick-off. Each side shall play an equal time from each In-Goal, and a match shall be won by a majority of points; if no point be scored, or the number be equal, the match shall be drawn.

NOTE. — The toss should be made in the presence of the Referee.

SCORING.

Scoring

The following shall be the mode of scoring:

A try shall equal three points.

A goal shall equal two points.

MODE OF PLAY.

Mode of Play

When once the ball is kicked off it may be kicked or picked up and run with by any player who is on-side, at any time; but it may not be picked up:—

(a) In a scrum

(b) When it is on the ground after a player has been tackled.

(c) When it has been put down after a tackle.

The ball may be passed or knocked from one player to another provided it be not passed, knocked, or thrown forward. If a player while holding or running with the ball be tackled, he must at once play the ball in accordance with note to "Tackle", - Law 2.

> *NOTE.— If a player is caught from behind he is not necessarily held because the tackler succeeds in getting his hands on the ball, unless the player's progress has been effectually stopped. On the other hand, if a player is tackled in front and held up, the tackler must instantly release his opponent, and the tackled player must at once play the ball.*

PLACED OFF-SIDE.

9. A player is placed off-side if the ball has been kicked, touched, or is being run with by one of his own side behind him. A player can be off-side in his opponents' in-goal, but not in his own, except where one of his side takes a free-kick behind his goal-line, in which case all his side must be behind the ball when kicked.

Placed Off-side

PLACED ON-SIDE

10. An off-side player, provided he is not within the 5 yards' limit, or engaged in a "play the ball" is placed on-side:
    (a) When an opponent has run 5 yards with the ball.

Placed On-side

(b) When the ball has been kicked or played by an opponent.

(c) When one of his side has run in front of him with the ball.

(d) When one of his side has run in front of him, having kicked the ball when behind him.

NOTE.— A player must be in the field-of-play when he puts his men on-side after kicking the ball when behind them. Whilst he is not debarred from following up in-touch, he must get into the field-of-play as soon as possible. It must be observed that only the kicker can place off-side players on-side.

An off-side player standing within the 5 yards' limit cannot under any circumstances be placed on-side.

Penalties for Off-side

An off-side player shall not play the ball, or actively or passively obstruct an opponent, or may not approach within 5 yards of any opponent waiting for the ball. On any breach of this law, except in the case of unintentional off-side, when a scrum shall be formed where such breach occurred, the opposite side shall be awarded at their option:—

(e) A penalty kick the place of such breach being taken as the mark.

(f) A scrum at the spot where the ball

was last played by the offending side before such breach occurred.

NOTE.— It is important that Referees should enforce these penalties, and should not readily give offending players the benefit of unintentional off-side instead of inflicting the full penalty.

FREE-KICKS AND PENALTY-KICKS

11. If a player makes and claims a fair-catch, his side shall be awarded a free-kick. Free-Kicks and Penalty-Kicks may be taken at any spot behind the mark in a line parallel to the touch lines. In all cases the kicker's side must be behind the ball when it is kicked. In case of any infringement the Referee shall order a scrum at the mark. The opposite side may come up to and stand anywhere on or behind a line drawn through the mark and parallel to the goal-line, but must not charge, or raise their hands higher than their heads. Should the ball not reach the line of the mark the Referee shall order a scrum. If the defending players having taken up their position, do any act to distract the attention of the kicker before the kick has been taken, the Referee shall be empowered to allow another kick.

Free-Kicks and Penalty Kicks

The places of infringement shall be taken as the mark, except when a player is foully charged, or deliberately obstructed,

Places of Infringement

after he has got in his kick, in which case
the penalty kick shall be taken where the
ball drops if in the field-of-play, at a spot 5
yards in the field-of-play opposite to
where it crossed the touch-line if it drops
directly into touch.

IV. PENALTIES.

12. Penalty-kicks shall be awarded if
any player:-

    (a) Intentionally either handles the ball
or falls down in a scrum, or picks
the ball out of a scrum.
NOTE.— A Forward going
down on one knee in an
endeavour to hook the ball, shall
be deemed to have intentionally
fallen down in the scrum.

    (b) Wilfully puts the ball unfairly into
a scrum.

    (c) Not in a scrum, gets in a line with
any of his forwards before the ball
comes out of such scrum.

    (d) Exercises unnecessary delay in
putting the ball in a scrum.

    (e) Being in a scrum lifts a foot from
the ground before the ball has been
put in, or is about to be put in, or
attempts to hook with foot nearest
to where the ball is coming in.

    (f) Puts his foot across the opening in
the scrum on that side where the
ball is being put in.

(g) Illegally plays the ball, tackles,
    charges, or obstructs, as in Law 10.
    *NOTE.— Where the tackle is
    simultaneous with the parting of
    the ball, it is not an obstruction.*

(h) Not himself running at the ball,
    charges or obstructs an opponent
    not holding the ball.

(i) With his hands pulls or pushes an
    opponent running for or dribbling
    the ball.

(j) Makes a deliberate knock-on or
    throw-forward.

(k) Does not immediately get up and
    put the ball down in front of him
    on being tackled, as per Law 2.

(l) Being on the ground does not
    immediately get up before putting
    the ball down.
    *NOTE.— The object of subsection
    (l) is chiefly to prevent accidents
    which otherwise might be caused
    by players kicking at the ball
    before the man is properly on his
    feet.*

EXAMPLES:—

*When a player is tackled by an opponent, and
    both players go down to the ground, the
    tackler must immediately get up, and must
    not use the body of his opponent to assist
    him in doing so. He is then out of the game
    until the ball is put down, and must in no
    way obstruct until this has been done.*

The man tackled must retain possession of the

ball until he has regained his feet (which he should do without delay) when he must at once drop the ball on the ground in front of him. The ball is then in play, and may be played by either side but only with the foot.

If a player, after being tackled and brought down (the ball having come into contact with the ground) wilfully throws the ball away from him whilst still on the ground, he should be penalised under Rule 12, Clause (j), or in extreme cases under Rule 14. on the other hand, should the Referee be satisfied that the ball has escaped from the hold of a player or players accidentally, he should then order a scrum.

A scrum should also be ordered: —

(a) When a number of players go down to the ground together, and the Referee is of the opinion that continuation of play would be dangerous.

(b) In cases where a breach of rule is committed by both sides.

(c) When the Referee is unable definitely to decide which side is to blame for not "playing the ball".

> NOTE.— In order to prevent wrestling, etc., when a player is tackled the Referee shall indicate to the players his decision that the ball is "held" by giving verbal instructions to "play the ball".
>
> The Referee must refrain

whenever possible from ordering a scrum under (b) or (c) in a "play the ball". He must order the players to take up proper positions and "play the ball" correctly.

(m) Gets nearer than 3 yards to the player acting as half-back in a "play the ball" movement.

(n) Prevents an opponent getting up or putting the ball down.

(o) If any player wilfully and systematically endeavours to prevent the formation of a fair and properly formed scrum.

(p) Plays the ball off-side after a knock-on as in Law 17.

(q) Foul play of any kind.
NOTE.— Although a penalty-kick is given, the Referee should caution a player, or order him off the ground.

As the object of imposing penalties is to enforce the Laws, and to penalise wrong-doers, the Referee may refrain from putting the provisions of this law into effect in cases where he is satisfied that by enforcing them he would be giving an advantage to the opposing side.

Refraining Clause

V. GENERAL.— BALL IN TOUCH.

Ball in Touch 13. The ball is in touch when it or a player carrying it touches or crosses the touch-line, except that a ball crossing the touch-line in the air and dropping in the field-of-play shall not be considered to have been in touch. When the ball drops directly into touch, it shall (except in the case of a penalty-kick and when a player kicks the ball into touch in the direction of his own in-goal and thereby loses ground) be brought back and a scrum ordered at the spot from whence it was kicked; in all other cases it shall be taken into play 10 yards from and at right angles to the touch-line and there put down for a scrum.

KICK AT GOAL FROM TRY.

Kick at Goal 14. When a side has scored a try, the ball shall be brought from the spot where the try was gained into the field-of-play, in a line parallel to the touch-lines, such distance as the kicker thinks proper, and there placed for a kick at goal.

NOTE.— *The defending side must retire to the goal-line and remain stationary while the kick is taken. On any breach of this, and the kick at goal is unsuccessful, the Referee shall allow another kick.*

AWARDING OR DISALLOWING A TRY.

The Referee shall award a try if, in his opinion, one would undoubtedly have been obtained but for unfair play by the defending side, or encroachment of spectators. Or, he shall disallow a try and adjudge a touch-down if, in his opinion, a try would undoubtedly not have been gained but for unfair play by the attacking side. In case of a try so allowed, the kick at goal shall be taken at any point on a line parallel to the touch-lines, and passing through the spot where the ball was when such unfair play or encroachments took place. A player may, for the purpose of getting a try in a more favourable position, pick up a ball lying motionless over his opponents' goal-line.

Unfair Play: Awarding or Disallowing a Try

TACKLED IN-GOAL.

15. If a player when over the goal-line and in possession of the ball be tackled before the ball is grounded, a scrum, 5 yards from the goal-line, shall be ordered.

Tackled In-Goal

DROP-OUT.

16. After a touch-down, or if the ball after crossing the goal-line goes into touch-in-goal, or touches or crosses the dead-ball line, it shall be brought into play by means of a drop-out.

Drop-Out

KNOCK-ON, THROW FORWARD.

Knock-On,
Throw
Forward

17. When a player knocks-on or throws the ball forward, any player of the opposite side may play the ball, but should the player who knocks-on or throws the ball forward play the ball, it shall at once be brought back to where such knock-on or throw forward took place, and there put down for a scrum. If an off-side player deliberately plays a ball knocked-on by one of his own side, the opposite side shall be awarded a penalty kick. A player who accidentally knocks the ball on shall not be penalised if he obtains possession before it falls to the ground.

BALL DEAD IN IN-GOAL.

Ball Dead in
In-Goal

18. In all cases where the ball is made dead in In-Goal by a defending player after having last touched one of his own side in the field-of-play, or if a player should kick, pass, knock, or carry the ball across his own goal-line, which is thereby made dead, the ball shall be brought back and a scrum formed in the field-of-play at a spot 5 yards from where it crossed the goal-line. Under any other circumstances a player may touch-down in his own in-goal.

TRIPPING-UP, BOOTS, ETC.

19. Tripping-up shall not be allowed under any circumstances. No one wearing projecting nails or iron plates on any part of his boots or shoes shall be allowed to to play in a match. A player will not be allowed to play without boots or shoes.

Tripping-Up, Boots, etc

BALL TO BE PUT IN SCRUM BY DEFENDING SIDE.

20. It shall be imperative for the ball to be put into a scrum on the side upon which the referee is standing, and the ball shall be placed in the scrum by one of the defending side.
Note - At kick-off, or drop-out from half-way, the team kicking-off or dropping out is deemed to be the attacking side.

Ball to be put in Scrum

IRREGULARITIES IN IN-GOAL NOT OTHERWISE PROVIDED FOR.

21. In case of any law being infringed in In-Goal by the attacking side, a dead ball shall be allowed, but where such breach is committed by the defending side, a scrum shall be ordered 5 yards from the goal-line opposite to the spot where the breach occurred.

Irregularities in In-Goal not otherwise provided for

OTHER IRREGULARITIES NOT PROVIDED FOR.

Other Irregularities. Advantage Law

22. In case of any law being broken or any irregularity of play occurs not otherwise provided for, and any advantage is gained therefrom by the opposite side, the Referee shall allow the game to proceed, but if no advantage is gained by such side, and if no other procedure is provided, the ball shall be taken back to the place where the breach of the law or irregularity occurred and a scrum formed there.

23. Any Club raising an objection to the result of a match under any of the Laws of the Game, must do so in writing, to the Council and the opposing club within 3 days of the match. Such notice of objection definitely stating the points on which the objection is made and the Rules under which the same is made, together with a deposit of £5, must be posted to the Council and a copy of such objection sent to the opposing club on the day the objection is laid. The Council may decline to entertain any points outside such declarations, and the deposit or any part of it may be forfeited if the objection is considered frivolous.

If any club desires the ruling of the Council on any question under the Laws of the Game, in cases where there is no protest as to the result of a match, it may submit a question stating definitely the facts of the case without making any deposit.

Rugby Renegade

AFTERWORD

by JOHN RISMAN

From the age of around five, I was steeped in all things rugby league. In our house, we all went to the games together. I had a rugby ball in my hands most of the time and my brother, Bev, who is seven years older than me, was already beginning to make his mark in representative matches.

Ours was a very sporting family in many ways, not just in terms of league. My father and brother were keen golfers too, and I used to act as their ball boy. I was also an enthusiastic fisherman. After all, I had to do something with my spare time, as they were rugby daft and always off somewhere training or playing. Living in Cumberland, there were some terrific places to take a rod.

The first time I can really remember seeing my father play was towards the end of his illustrious career, at Wembley in 1952, when he sensationally led Workington to an 18-10 Challenge Cup victory against Featherstone.

I sat on mum's knee in those evocative surroundings,

taking in the game and especially the presentations. Then we went back to the hotel to meet and cheer the team. I can vividly recall having to stay in the bedroom with the trophy. I looked at it all night, picked it up and drank out of it; we knew that you weren't supposed to but everybody did and I couldn't resist it.

Afterwards, the Cup was kept at our house and I could immediately see and sense the charisma and standing that my father had in the community, which had culminated in that historic win. It was obvious that he was a well known and hugely respected man and that would always be the case.

As I started to grow up and the mischievous nature of a typical boy began to kick in, my father never had to clip me round the ear or resort to raising his voice because he had so many other sanctions available to him that taught me about life. One of his favourites, in the summer, if I'd overstepped the mark, came from the fact that we lived no more than three hundred metres from the River Cocker. He'd get me up at 6.30 in the morning. We'd run down to the river, go straight in for a swim and then run back. The Cocker is the fastest flowing river in Britain and drops the furthest from source to mouth, so to say it was fairly cold is an understatement. The feeling of it remains etched in the memory.

My father had greater priorities than talking about his halcyon days as one of the greatest rugby league players of all time. To us, he was just a normal dad, but he did have a trophy cabinet filled with some of his most prized possessions, most of which he had brought home from trips abroad with Great Britain.

There was an ostrich egg, a huge snake skin and a beautiful artefact from the 1936 tour - a boomerang signed by all the players which has the results of all the games written on it. These are now my own treasured personal effects and cherished items of memorabilia, handed down through the generations, and they mean a lot to me.

The Risman household was very calm. My father always had a certain dignity and posture about him and his answers to any question were measured. There was no losing of temper. Every problem was talked through and dealt with, without any hassle. It was a wonderful time and environment in which to grow up.

I'm sure that he would have adopted that same, assured attitude with his players; he did not have to shout to be heard, his character and personality would have carried that before him. If that is the way he came across and how he got the best out of his team then, as his offspring, you have to be immensely proud.

In many ways, my own character is very similar to his. I have had the opportunity to work in developing areas, new to the sport and often overseas. As such, I tend to do a lot of coaching where clear communication is the key. I myself first signed as a professional player in 1970 and, since then, have worked in the game for nearly forty years as either a player or coach at various levels and in different surroundings. It is important to have a high level of love and affection for the code and a certain patience and understanding if you are going to try and make an impact and leave a legacy in places like Serbia and Latvia, where rugby league is not second nature, as it was to me when growing up.

Such development - almost missionary - work is the kind of thing that I love doing, because rugby league has been and continues to be my life. There is also a certain irony that my father's background is closely linked to Eastern Europe, an area of the world to which I have had the privilege of helping to introduce the code in recent seasons.

My grandfather on my father's side died in 1931, way

before I was born, so our Latvian heritage never came to light, really. My father's Welsh background was the more dominant cultural force in our lives. Having coached Latvia, for me, that part of the family history has now come more into perspective. On the other side, we were predominantly Scottish and, again, I have had the pleasure and privilege to work with the flower of that nation's youth at various levels, which has also meant a lot to me coaching-wise.

Overall, the Risman roots are a mixture of the Eastern – Latvian and Russian - and Celtic – Scots and Welsh. Through my involvement with rugby league, I now intend to find out even more about who I am and the ancestors who helped to shape the character of my father, a true sporting giant.

As told to PHIL CAPLAN

Available now or coming soon from Scratching Shed Publishing Ltd...

Last of the Dinosaurs
The Kevin Ashcroft Story - by Maurice Bamford

Last of the Dinosaurs charts the eventful, brutal & often controversial career of Kevin Ashcroft - a man thought by many to be the first truly modern rugby league hooker. Awash with incident and anecdote, this is an entertaining read, detailing Ashcroft's stints with Warrington, Leigh, Salford, Dewsbury & Rochdale among much else.

OUT NOW ISBN: 9780956007520

Tries & Prejudice
Ikram Butt, with Tony Hannan

The revealing, hard-hitting and often amusing autobiography of former Featherstone, Leeds and London rugby star Ikram Butt. Born and bred in Leeds and, these days, the driving force behind BARA - the British Asian Rugby Association - England's first muslim rugby international tells his unique life story, whilst also offering an insight into the muslim experience of British sport.

PUBLISHED SPRING 2009

Turned Out Nice Again
A History of Northern Comedy - Tony Hannan

From music hall to the world wide web, from George Formby Senior to Peter Kay, Great Britain has long mined the north of England for its comedians. Yet, as this entertaining and definitive volume on the subject reveals, far from being a mere off-shoot of English humour, northern comedy has consistently been at its very heart.

PUBLISHED AUTUMN 2009

COVER
CURRENTLY
UNAVAILABLE

Scratching Shed Publishing Ltd

Scratching Shed Publishing Ltd is an independent publishing company founded in May 2008. We aim to produce high-quality books covering a range of subjects - including sport, travel and popular culture - of worldwide interest yet with the distinctive flavour of the North of England.